Playing With Pain

Stories from My Life in Leather

First Edition

Hardy Haberman

Playing With Pain

Pain

Stories from My Life in Leather

First Edition

Published by The Nazca Plains Corporation
Las Vegas, Nevada
2007

ISBN: 978-1-934625-17-0

Published by

The Nazca Plains Corporation ®
4640 Paradise Rd, Suite 141
Las Vegas NV 89109-8000

PUBLISHER'S NOTE
Playing With Pain is a work of fiction created wholly by *Hardy
Haberman's* imagination. All characters are fictional and any
resemblance to any persons living or deceased is purely by accident.
No portion of this book reflects any real person or events.

Cover, Hardy Haberman
Art Director, Blake Stephens

**Dedicated to
My Mother and Father**

Playing With Pain

Stories from My Life in Leather

Hardy Haberman

Contents

Introduction

When you are only 3 years old, it doesn't take a lot to amuse you. For me, sitting on the lawn, pulling up tufts of grass while my mother hung up freshly washed clothes was activity enough to keep me quiet for a while. But it didn't take long before I was scouting the yard for new playthings.

I watched my mother as she pulled wooden clothespins from a tattered pink cloth bag and clipped them to the billowing white sheets she hung on the clothesline. Seeing the sheets flap in the gentle Texas breeze held my attention for a few more minutes, but something more interesting caught my eye. A couple of clothespins had fallen to the ground, and in an instant I had them firmly in hand.

These were simple devices. Two slats of wood and a spring, but squeezing them open and snapping them closed delighted me. My mother, noticing this fascination, pulled a few more pins from the bag and clipped them to her apron, then handed me the remaining bag. I am sure she included an admonishment to "be careful with them" but I was transfixed by the sight of so many little wooden clips.

It wasn't long before I had them all out of the bag, lining them up on the ground like soldiers. Knocking them over like rows of dominos, and finally, finding places to clip them. Soon my shirt was festooned with them, they rattled as I moved and this delighted me even more. Then, I performed one simple act of experimentation. It was one of those acts only children do, but its effects were profound. Little did I know that I would be shaping my future with something so simple?

I opened one of the clothespins and clipped it to the fold of skin between my thumb and forefinger. Looking at it hanging there, I began to feel the growing sensation as the spring squeezed my flesh tighter and tighter. Tears were welling up in my eyes, but I couldn't stop looking at the pin dangling from my skin. I shook my hand to see if it would relieve the pain. It did not seem to make any difference. I pulled at the pin, but stopped when the pain increased as the rough wood abraded my skin.

I guess most children my age would have either screamed for Mommy, or simply opened the clothespin and taken it off, but something else was going through my mind. I didn't want it to come off. It hurt, but not that bad, and it was interesting, and the pain was going away. It really wasn't too bad at all. Before long, I had clothespins hanging from every finger and the spaces in between.

It was my boisterous laughing that got my mother's attention. She looked down and saw me there, hands covered in clothespins and she gasped. Reaching down, she scooped me up and quickly pulled the pins off my hand. That's when I cried. Everywhere she removed a pin; it felt like my skin was on fire.

After that I don't remember much, except that I learned a valuable lesson. The pain I experienced when I put the pins on myself was welcome pain. It came from an activity that I understood and was inflicted at a pace that I controlled. It was a "good ouch". The pain I felt when my mother removed the clothespins, was unwelcome pain. I didn't expect it and had no control over it. It was a "bad ouch".

It's been over 50 years since that spring day in Texas, and I still play with clothespins. Funny how some things never change.

That difference between "good" and "bad" pain is what SM is all about. The effects on the body from welcome or "good" pain is the root of ecstatic experience, and though it is not always the result, for me that ecstatic experience is always the goal. I like taking people on a journey to a peak experience that, for my tastes, only SM can bring.

I get enormous pleasure out of guiding a partner through the experience and helping them emerge on a plateau of heightened sensation. There they can lose the last vestiges of ego and become a primal, ecstatic being.

OK, so it sounds a little hokey, but it's about the only way to describe what happens. When the person I am playing with moves beyond their struggle against the sensation and lets the waves of pain bathe them. When their voices turn from groans of discomfort to guttural animalistic moans. When their whole body shakes with orgasmic tremors, which is the peak experience I strive for.

They are not alone on their journey. I am there with them, feeling and responding to their reactions in a similar fashion. Riding their ecstasy along with them, I too get caught up in the primal sensation. I am panting, sweating and shaking almost as much as they are, drawing energy from the mere proximity of our bodies, exhilarated from the experience.

Afterward, it takes me almost as much time to "come down" from a really good scene as the partner I am playing with. If we both have made that connection, we have shared that ecstasy and also a connection that is more on the spiritual level than physical.

Do all my scenes end this way? No. But when they do it is always a memorable experience, and the more I work to perfect my technique, exploring new methods and theories, the better my scenes become. That is what this is all about, exploring and learning. As practitioners of SM, we are essentially explorers. We build on the experiences of our mentors and forbears, and constantly innovate and try new things. That's a big part of the fun!

We are sexual pioneers, and as such are always on the frontier of what is possible and practical. It is not always what we expect, but it is always interesting, and that's why it appeals to me. There are no hard and fast rules, only guidelines that keep my partners and me safe.

Why pain? For me the reason is simple. Controllable, consensual pain is a short cut to a kind of intimacy that I enjoy. It's also something that is enjoyable for the people I play with. In the vanilla world it isn't often that you use the words "pain" and "enjoy" in the same sentence, but in the world of SM it's an everyday occurrence. Kinky folk understand the principals behind pain and how it relates to pleasure. It is a connection that has only recently been confirmed by scientific research. In fact the researchers who confirmed this connection even postulated in an interview that, perhaps this is the reason so many people involved in Sadomasochism enjoy the activities. I suspect this will be the only time this collation will ever be acknowledged in a scientific context; however I would love to help craft a research project to explore that further.

Throughout the remainder of this book, I will delve into the techniques I use for inducing controlled pain, and the delights it can achieve. I encourage the reader to explore and discover on his or her own, this is only a starting point. I also encourage the reader who chooses to explore the pain/pleasure continuum, to learn as much as he or she can about how to play safely and how to effectively negotiate a scene with any potential partner.

In the process I hope to give a little insight into my own journey, including true stories that should give the reader an idea of how these techniques work in the real world.

Safety

Though several volumes have been written about safety in regard to SM play it never hurts to review. My first personal rule is pretty simple, when it doubt, err on the side of caution. My second rule is similarly simple; if I don't understand the risks of a certain kind of play, learn them. I know I will rarely go wrong being cautious and educated.

Most of the play that I do involving pain carries a few risks. To me, these risks seem minor, but to someone else they might be well within the realm of "Edge Play". (Play that carries a higher potential risk) So once again, let me define a few terms and levels of risk before I go on.

First the term "risk" can have many definitions. Risk, for me, means that there is a potential for some kind of physical harm that might be unintended during play.

Additionally, I like to take into consideration the possibility of psychological or emotional harm. An activity might be relatively safe, but it might hit a hot button for a partner emotionally or psychologically.

For example, I was doing a pre-negotiated spanking scene with a submissive partner or "bottom" who had never experienced it before. Half-way through the scene, he began weeping uncontrollably and I decided to stop the scene even though he had not used his "safe word". He had never considered that some repressed memories of childhood physical abuse would surface while bent over my knee, but something opened that door in his mind and now he was suffering a wave of pent up grief and anger from the experience. I did my best to comfort him until he regained his composure. Not being a psychologist, I did not try to council him about his problems, I simply listened to him and helped him de-compress from the experience. Had I been more thorough in my negotiation I might have been able to anticipate this reaction and avoid the activity, but even he did not expect his reaction. Had we been doing something else other than spanking it might have never happened.

As long as we both understood the possible risks involved and were willing to do what was necessary to cope with anything that might come up then there was nothing we could have done differently. However, if as a Top or bottom I am not willing to take responsibility for something going wrong, and prepare to deal with that eventuality, then I have no business playing in that realm.

The same is true for physical risks as well. If I am going to play at an activity that could cause harm, I need to know how to deal with it should it happen. This includes a working knowledge of CPR as well as minor first aid. It's just common sense. After all, you wouldn't jump off a diving board into a pool if you didn't know how deep the water was and whether or not you could swim!

I'll discuss some safety issues for specific kinds of play later on, as well as the risks associated with each kind of activity.

Now for the big disclaimer:

> *Anyone undertaking any activity described in this book, does so at his or her own risk. I am assuming we are all adults here, and as adults we are responsible for our own actions. Just because you read a story about someone jumping off a cliff and surviving without a scratch, you don't go out and try to duplicate that experience. If you do, you are in serious need of therapy, or will be once you crash to the ground and break several bones. In this age of "Jackass" there are going to be people who will try anything and often without any consideration of the consequences. Every action has consequences! Use common sense and safety precautions whenever doing anything that has a potential for physical or psychological harm.*

For now I hope you enjoy these stories of my experiences in the world of leather and specifically my fascination with all the aspects of intense sensation...pain. With any luck, the experience will not be painful for you, at least the reading part.

The Pain/Pleasure Continuum

I am not a physiologist, so take any pronouncements I make with enough salt for your taste. I have come to understand pain as a combination of intense sensations, specifically those that stimulate the "pain response" systems of the body.

These sensations can come from a variety of physical causes: heat, cold, pressure, percussion, electro-stimulation or invasive activities including piercing or cutting.

These kinds of stimulus are controllable and can be applied with a certain amount of precision, and that makes them appropriate for use in an SM scene. Pain caused by internal organs, disease, or other cause is not the kind of pain we play with in SM. Those kinds of pain are usually beyond our control unless you are using artificial methods like anesthesia or drugs. Save that for doctors!

Every day we experience many if not all of these sensations, yet few people would consider them painful. I believe that whether a sensation is considered painful or not is largely a subjective matter. For example you see a friend you haven't seen in years. You greet him and give him a hearty slap on the back. It's an endearing gesture and to most it would not be painful, unless you had a previous injury to your back.

That same slap could be considered painful if it was given in a different circumstance. If you don't believe this, let me give you another example from my childhood. My parents were taking me to the amusement park for a day of fun. As I fooled around before leaving, my father gave me a playful slap on the bottom to encourage me to get a move on and get in the car. I jumped up into the back seat and we were off for a day of fun. Later that night, I protested leaving the park so soon. Again, he swatted me on the butt, and probably no more forcefully that before, but this time I cried. Sobbing on the way home, I doubt if I was considering the subjectivity of the sensation but today I can.

I interpreted the first swat as playful and fun. The second swat was interpreted as discipline and not fun. Same sensation, two different experiences. Now, there were different circumstances accompanying both swats, but still it was my subjective interpretation that made the difference.

I call the two types of interpretation as welcome pain and unwelcome pain. It is the difference between a "good ouch" and a "bad ouch". For those unfamiliar with hose terms let me explain.

> Good Ouch - Getting an erotic spanking while bent over a padded bench.

> Bad Ouch – Getting poked by a loose staple holding the padding onto the bench.

The welcome pain was the spanking; the unwelcome pain was the poke by the staple.

Not every case is as clear cut, but you get the general idea. The definition of pleasure is a little trickier, but again it is subjective.

Here is an example from my household. My boy and I have three cats. One cat absolutely loves being stroked from head to tail. She will purr and nuzzle for hours while you stroke her. Another cat tolerates stroking only on her head and neck. Touch her tail and you will receive a sharp rebuke in the form of a bite. Both cats perceive the strokes as pleasurable, they purr when you do it, but where they perceive it as pleasurable is different. Neither have any physical problem that would make the strokes painful, but their subjective judgment of what is nice and what is not could not be clearer.

Feline quirks aside, the same kinds of definitions work for people. Pleasurable activities include listening to music, watching movies, playing games, physical recreation, sexual activities, creative pursuits, and more. However, every item on this list is subject to personality and interpretations.

For example, some people are brought to the brink of ecstasy by classical music, while some municipalities actually use piped in classical music to drive away panhandlers and gang members. Riding a bicycle can be one person's idea of a pleasurable activity but for me it is tantamount to torture. Pleasure is again a subjective perception.

There are few clear cut lines between pain and pleasure, and in recent medical research it looks like the same centers in the brain are stimulated by both sensations. This really blurs the line between pain and pleasure, and it is in this blur that the SM practitioner plays.

Depending on the circumstance a lot of activities that might be painful can be pleasurable. Remember the clothespins? When little Hardy started putting more and more clothespins on his skin, he triggered the body's pain defense. Specifically the sensation was detected by nociceptors, the nerve endings in the skin. These receptors detect temperature, pressure or chemical activity that could be damaging to the skin or organs they surround. That defense or reflex is a natural process whereby the body tries to either escape the pain or mitigate it by manufacturing opioids. These chemicals bind to opioid receptors in the central nervous system and relieve the pain.

Some of the best known ones are endorphins, natural opioids that produce analgesia and a sense of well being. It is the chemical that produces the much touted "runner's high", and it's one of the main reasons some SM activities are fun.

Endorphins are one of the reasons, but not the only reason. The other is arousal that comes from the sex organ between your ears. Your brain interprets things that are happening to you and can kick in other chemicals that make the pain not only pleasurable but sexy.

If you were to be thrown into a real dungeon during the Inquisition and flogged, you probably would get some relief from endorphins, but unless you are a real sick puppy you would not be sexually aroused. That same activity in a modern SM dungeon can be great foreplay to a night of wild and rough sex! In the SM sense it is welcome pain, whereas administered by Torquemada the Grand Inquisitor, its torture.

This is where the magic of SM comes in. I sincerely believe people who enjoy SM are gifted. We have been given the gift of transformation. We can take something that most people would consider frightening and embrace it as foreplay. We transform sensations most people would find painful into cathartic intimate release. It does sound a little like magic, doesn't it?

Bondage is almost universally considered a restrictive and undesirable condition. To an SM enthusiast, bondage can be freedom itself. Being bound, gagged or restrained can trigger a state where the mind can fanaticize and the body can respond almost apart from consciousness. Bondage can give psychological "permission" to experience sensations and activities that otherwise would seem unthinkable.

For example, Ruth is a powerful woman. She is an executive with many responsibilities and skilled at handling tough business negotiations. She also enjoys SM, and in the dungeon she absolutely loves being tied up with rope in elaborate bondage play. While tied up she has often been ordered to lick her Master's boots. As Ruth, the businesswoman, she would never be able to do this or derive any pleasure at all from it. But as Ruth, the submissive woman tied in a kneeling position in the dungeon, licking her Masters boots is not only pleasurable for her, it is a sign of her gratitude for the hard work her Master put into the elaborate rope bondage. The bondage gave her "permission" to set aside her ego and allow herself to engage in what would otherwise be a humiliating act. Later that night, Ruth and her Master (also known as her husband) will go home and have wild sex. For that she requires no permission!

A whip is usually considered an instrument of torture and suffering, but in the hands of a skilled SM Top it becomes a sex toy. The intense stings of the whip as it grazes the skin can bring waves of deep sensation that releases floods of not only natural opioids, but emotions as well. A good single-tail whip scene can be almost as ecstatic as an orgasm for some bottoms.

Our ability to transcend the traditional experiences and mold them into sensual ones is the magic I am talking about. It is what keeps me returning again and again to the dungeon. Transcendence is what lifts what we, as SM participants, do from the realm of just kinky play to something more. In fact it's not uncommon for people who have had a really intense scene to describe it with spiritual terms. It is spiritual in a sense, because each person in the scene has shared something deeply intimate with each other. That sharing goes beyond mere communication or simple sexual arousal. It touches something deep and universal in every participant's soul. That connection is where the spiritual experience happens.

The line between pain and pleasure is not a firm barrier it is more of a continuum. As I said earlier it's subjective. One day you can really be ready for a great deal of pain and the next you may not. Time plays a big factor. For many people, SM play occurs only in the evening. This is not only because that's when they have free time, but it may be when their internal clock is set for sexual activities. The old designation of being a morning or evening person holds true for SM as well.

An all-men's play group I belong to has parties on Sunday afternoons. For some members of the group, this is very difficult. Their internal clocks are set for a later time, and for them the parties never get as hot as private play in the evening. For me, I like mornings. My boy and I often play on weekend mornings before we start our day. Some studies indicate that this internal clock may also be affected by the natural opioids produced by the body. Specifically, dynorphin is implicated in this process in a study published in the Journal *Science,* January 1983.

The pain and pleasure line may also be affected by other factors such as fatigue, nutrition and stress. No matter what the reason, the key thing to remember is that the pain/pleasure continuum is not a rigid structure and it can change. SM players need to always remain flexible and most of all responsive to their partners condition. That means good communication not only before a scene but during it and after as well.

The time spent after a scene is a prime opportunity to debrief both Top and bottom. It is a great time to let each other know what worked and what you would have liked done differently. I am not saying you should immediately critique a scene the moment it is over, but during the cool-down and aftercare the players can open the channel of communication. Sometimes it may take days before you fully process what worked and what didn't during a scene, and that should be taken into account. Touching base with your play partner a couple of days later is a good idea, especially if you do not live with him or her on a full time basis.

Before I get too far afield from the topic at hand let me suggest that if you are interested in more information on dungeon etiquette or SM in general, read Jay Wiseman's *SM 101*. It offers a great overview of the scene and is a good place to start for anyone exploring the kink scene. Additionally, I always like to refer my readers to the groundbreaking book by the late Geoff Mains, *Urban Aboriginals*. In it he gives a detailed account of the brain activity surrounding the pain/pleasure continuum as well as a great history of gay leathersex.

Let me reprise something I wrote in my earlier book, *More Family Jewels*. To understand the pain/pleasure continuum in a graphic way, consider a circle. The top arc represents pain and the bottom arc represents pleasure. The dividing line between the two arcs is not fixed, rather it moves constantly because of many of the factors already discussed. To try to fix a specific point on the circumference of the circle is equally difficult, so we can only find general areas that can be clearly identified

Pain

Pleasure

as absolute pain or pleasure.

It is perhaps no accident that the Taoist symbol "taijitu", the yin and yang looks like this circle. It represents the passive and active, the dark and light, the feminine and masculine. To see this, as a dichotomy with one force being superior to the other is a Western view, the Eastern view is that each exists as a cyclical process, integral to each other and is interdependent. SM is based on the give and take, the dichotomy of pain and pleasure and the absolute interdependence of both.

Here's an example I witnessed at a private party that might help explain the pain/pleasure continuum better. The couple, a very attractive man and woman wanted me to help out in the man's first mummification scene. For those who don't know, mummification is a sensory depravation scene that in this case involved the bottom being wrapped in layers of plastic wrap and duct tape.

To begin he undressed, while his girlfriend and I prepared the area we intended to play in. We used a massage table, a large roll of industrial plastic wrap and a couple of rolls of duct tape. We also had a pair of bandage scissors to cut him out once the scene was over.

To minimize sweating, once he was naked, we put towels under his arms and between his legs. Then we began slowly wrapping his body from his feet upward in plastic wrap. We made sure it wasn't too tight to prevent cutting off blood circulation. We continued wrapping his body in plastic, encasing his arms and chest and finally wrapping his head and neck, being sure to not cover his mouth and nose. We wanted him to be able to breathe easily, and to be able to communicate if needed.

Once he was fully wrapped, we began using strips of duct tape to encase the plastic wrap. This is a long process and it takes a methodical Top. As each strip of tape covered more and more of his body, his breathing became more even and he settled into a very calm and relaxed state. That reaction is common during a mummification. Bottoms often speak of the feeling as a floating or an out-of-body experience.

Once he was fully covered, again with the exception of his nose and mouth, we moved him to the massage table face up, and we let him drift for a while. We kept watching closely for his breathing and to make sure he was OK.

Some people like to be mummified and just drift for a long time, others like things a little more spicy, and that's what was going to happen tonight. We carefully used the bandage scissors to make a small incision just above his pubic area, and then carefully cut a hole exposing his cock and balls only. The operative word here is carefully!

Once the tape and plastic were removed from his pubic area, his cock sprang to attention through the hole. Though he was deprived of many sensations, his mind turned the scene into one of intense sexual arousal. Also, the sudden exposure of the skin on his genitals contributed to the arousal. It focused his mind on them as well.

We began by gently teasing his penis and testicles with our fingers and a few sensation toys. She had brought a feather duster, which though extremely gentle, can be very effective when the body is aroused and receptive to sensations. The tips of the feather duster moving up and down the erect shaft of his penis made his whole body twitch and writhe inside the cocoon of duct tape.

After suitable teasing she produced a tube of lube and began to work in earnest on his hard cock. Using her lubricated hand, she stroked his penis in a slow methodical manner. He responded immediately. The warm hand and slippery lube really focused his energies on his penis. I gently massaged his tightening balls as she stroked him. We were careful to not touch him in any other way. By doing this we forced him to concentrate only on his genitals and heightened the sensation.

After what seemed like hours, I could tell he was getting very close to ejaculation. His scrotum had contracted and his penis was twitching wildly. He bucked his whole body beneath our hands as if desperate for other contact. Finally he could take no more and began to ejaculate. His orgasm was spectacular, and his semen shot what seemed like a couple of feet into the air.

So far, though intense, everything we had done would pretty much be considered pleasurable, however that was all about to change. Once he had finished ejaculating, we did not let up on our actions. I kept fondling and she kept stroking and his body began bucking again. He began groaning loudly and then began begging us to stop. Since he did not use his prearranged safe word, we continued as though he had not spoken at all.

His begging became more and more insistent as the pleasurable activity of being stroked now became torture. His penis and nerve endings were over-stimulated and what had once been fun was now painful. To add to his discomfort she began to rub her hand over the extra sensitive head of his penis. This brought howls and finally his safe word.

So what happened? Well, what started as welcome sensation became unwelcome sensation. So unwelcome, that he had to call the scene to a halt. Now, let me assure you that when we brought him out of the mummy wrap, he was delighted and thanked us both profusely. Though the sensations had gone from pleasurable to painful, overall, they were enjoyable and therefore a good thing.

So you can see by this example that pain and pleasure have few rigid boundaries and can change depending on the situation and mood of the people involved. That is one of the key things to remember when playing with intense sensations and pain. As a Top you must remain responsive to the reactions of the person bottoming to you and as a bottom you must be communicative with the Top. Otherwise things can get out of control quickly and what could have been a very hot scene can become a dud or worse, a nightmare.

A Day at the Fair –
All the World is a Stage

It's a pilgrimage for me. Every year since I was old enough to walk I go to the State Fair of Texas. At first it was as a toddler being tugged along by my parents but later I made the journey on my own. Each year the local schools gave out free tickets to the Fair and gave students a day off to attend. In later years, sometime around my 12th birthday, I even got to go to the Fair without my parents as chaperones.

So why was this so important? Well, without their watchful eyes, I was free to ride any ride or see any show I wanted. This was a big deal. Today, fair midways have lots of rides and food and games, but what are missing are the shows. Back then, there were shows, lots of them. At the back end of the midway, stood the show tents, their facades festooned with colorful banners, signs and lights. Out front there was always a stage, later I learned this was called the "bally". On the bally performers from the shows would give the crowds a preview of what they would see on the inside.

The biggest crowds formed around the stages of two shows on the midway. One was the "Cotton Club Review". This was an all-black musical revue with lots of musicians and of course lots of girls in skimpy outfits. It was a given that my friends and I would be seeing this show, something we could never do with our parents along.

The other big draw on the midway was the sideshow. The banners outside promised that in this tent we would be treated to a congress of the world's most unusual people. My parents certainly would never allow me in there, so that's where I went as soon as I reached the midway.

I bought my ticket and scurried inside where I was told by the "talker" outside that the show was going on "right now"! I paid for my ticket and hurried inside the tent. What I had expected was a theatre arrangement with rows of seats and a stage. Instead there were several stages, spread out along the length of the tent and the audience moved from stage to stage as the show progressed.

I arrived just in time to see a man with very small hands instead of arms and apparently no legs, only abbreviated appendages he called "flippers". This was Sealo the Seal Boy. He was hardly a boy, appearing to be somewhere around his mid 50's, and he didn't look like a seal, just a profoundly deformed man. Sealo was jolly enough, he laughed and made jokes and did a few "tricks" which were amazing only because it would seem impossible that someone without arms or legs could light a cigarette, much less roll it from scratch.

The next act was the "Torture King". He was what appeared to be just a normal man, with the exception of his extensive tattoos. Later I found out he was also the "Tattooed Wonder". It seemed that everyone in the sideshow did at least two acts.

The Torture King explained that he had studied in India the ways of the mysterious fakirs and also spent years learning the mysteries of the Hindu Yogis. Today, he would be demonstrating one of those mysteries to our "amazed eyes". I pushed closer. Since I was an amateur magician I wanted to get a good look at what I expected to be real magic.

TK removed his shirt, revealing the amazing canvas of his chest and back. He was covered in illustrations like a page out of an illuminated manuscript. The soft colors and lines blended into a garment of tattoo that he wore permanently. Somewhere deep down inside, I felt a tingle. Not only did his skin fascinate me, but also his musculature stirred my burgeoning sexuality. I had not had much experience observing naked men, even if it was only from the waist up. Add that to the fact that he openly invited the audience to look at his skin and I was getting goose bumps.

On the platform was a wooden cover. It was flat and about 5 feet long. TK reached down and pulled the cover up, revealing a board bristling with shining steel nails. The audience gasped. TK explained that there were over 700 stainless steel nails on the board and he proceeded to demonstrate their sharpness by tossing a potato into the air. The spud landed on the board with a thump, it was completely impaled on the sharp nails. This brought another gasp and the crowd moved even closer, pushing me to the edge of the stage.

From this vantage point I felt almost intimate with the Torture King as he knelt before the bed of nails. He explained that Indian Fakirs would defy the laws of physics through the mysterious powers of yoga and risk life and limb in a test of their faith. With that he asked for silence. I was breathless as I watched him sit on the edge of the board and slowly lay down until his full back was directly atop the threatening nails. Once he was in position, the announcer, stepped up on the platform and announced that not only would the Torture King withstand the nails, but the additional weight of a member of the audience. His hand pointed at me, and like a sleepwalker I walked up the steps to the stage.

The announcer put a small piece of plywood on TK's chest and then asked me to step up slowly onto the board. I was shaking as I took the first tentative step. All of a sudden, TK let out a scream. Luckily I had not had anything to drink yet, otherwise I would have provided a bonus show for the audience. His scream was all part of the act, and once the laughter subsided, the announcer told me to take a bow for helping. TK then rose from the bed of nails and turned to display his back, covered in small indentions, but not a drop of blood! He even encouraged me to touch his skin to see if there were any holes.

By the time I got down from the stage, the audience had moved to the next attraction, and that was just as well. I had developed what I later learned was an erection and was feeling giddy and embarrassed.

What I found so interesting about the Torture King's performance was not only his amazing skin, but also the act of lying on what must have been a painful device and still come up smiling. Though I didn't know it at the time, TK was smiling partially from the chemical stew that was rushing through his body. No he wasn't on drugs. He was high from natural opioids that were stimulated by the act of lying on the sharp points of the nails.

Once I had arrived home from the Fair, I asked my father about the bed of nails, and he explained that it was simple physics not a mysterious power that kept TK from being harmed. One or two nails supporting the weight of a full grown human would stab through the skin as easily as the nails had pierced the potato. Spread over the entire back at a spacing of about one nail every square inch, and it would take the weight of several men to do any damage. That explanation was one of the advantages of having a scientist for a father! The downside was I had admitted I was in the sideshow and that took a lot more explanation but this time to my mother.

Since that day, the effects of that act intrigued me. As an adult I have actually built and used my own bed of nails and can attest from experience it is relatively safe and effective. Its effectiveness becomes evident once the initial discomfort goes away and the body begins producing the natural opioids that ease pain.

Though I don't have a scientific study to back it up, from what I can tell the bed of nails plays a trick on the brain. The numerous points of discomfort start a process that overloads the brains pain control activities and this triggers the body to produce an overabundance of endorphins. It is those that cause the "high" which comes from an extended "nap" on the bed of nails. It is the same kind of high that a runner gets when they run a marathon, or that a bottom gets during a flogging or whip scene.

Beyond the science, I found the entire act extremely sexy and I suspect now that it was because of the pleasure/pain aspect of the performance that I was aroused. As a burgeoning Sadist, seeing people enduring pain willingly was a turn-on.

I have used my bed of nails during workshops and with play partners in a more intimate setting. It still has the power to elicit gasps from observers. At one national conference, as I lay down on the nails and had a friend stand on my chest I overheard two comments. "Oh my God, that has to hurt!" and "damn that is sexy". Both are true.

The feeling is not so much painful as profoundly annoying, at least until my body gets used to it. Once I am settled and the natural opioids start to flow the feeling is one of almost levitation. The nails seem to go away and I am floating on a sea of sensation. It is that mystical experience that I suppose made the bed of nails a genuine feature of Hindu mystics' ascetic routines.

How the body feels sensations on the back has a lot to do with this as well. The nerve endings which register pressure on the back are spread out more than on other body parts. Because of this sensitivity on the back is less precise than on the hand for example. In fact, the nerve endings are so widely spaced; you can play a trick on your back. Get a compass or calipers, and set it o a distance of 1" in width. Then touch someone's back with first one point and the both points. (Lightly!)

In most cases the person you are touching will not be able to tell the difference between the single point and the pair. You will have to spread the calipers almost 2.5" before the nerves on the back can tell the difference. This inability to register accurate information on the back makes the bed of nails less painful as well.

> *For the record, I do not advocate anyone just going out and building a bed of nails. Thought you might be successful, you might also find yourself badly injured. It took quite a bit of tinkering before I found the right spacing and arrangement of the nails before I was successful.*

Now if you just absolutely have to experience it, you and a friend can make a trip to your local office supply store and buy a plastic rolling chair mat. These are backed with hundreds of pints that keep them from sliding on a carpeted floor. If the points are spaced on 1" centers you should be turn the mat over and lie down on the bottom side safely. Don't wiggle or try to slide across the points, they will cut you!

Also when you get up, have your friend available to help you off should you become uncomfortable or unable to get up. Don't do this alone!

Another thing that made the whole experience so sexy was the exhibitionism of it. Though I do not consider myself to be an exhibitionist (I don't have an Adonis-like body), I do like to show off. Throughout my life I have sought to do things that brought me in front of an audience, and to that extent I am guilty. The sideshow aspect of some SM activities fascinates me. Their very sensationalism is what makes them sexy for me. The bed of nails is one of those things.

Though it can be fun to play with alone or with a single partner, for me it is even more fun in a dungeon or public playspace. I guess I never got over hearing the gasps and the applause that day at the fair.

For a Top in the dungeon or other public playspace, there is always the matter of observers. That audience can either heighten or distract from the scene. Part of that result is directly the responsibility of the Dungeon Monitors at the event. DM's are people whose primary job is the safety and well being of the participants at an event. DM's are often trained in first-aid and CPR, as well as basic dungeon safety and more importantly, crowd control. A really hot scene in a dungeon often draws a big crowd of watchers. This in itself is not a problem, but when it becomes too big or too noisy, it can totally ruin a scene.

For me as well as many other Tops I know, public scenes have the potential to be even more fun than private ones. I think that comes from a couple of important things. Because of their nature, public scenes (and I am talking about scenes in a consensual space) are by their nature exhibitionistic. The Top and bottom get to show off a little and that adds to the titillation. For a Top this may be heightened by the idea that so many people may be admiring his technique. For a bottom it may come from the thought that so many people are seeing them in a position of submission, etc. There are a host of subtle reasons that can make the exhibitionistic aspect of a scene hot for the players involved. For me it is a combination of feeding my ego and knowing that others are enjoying the scene as well.

The second thing that makes a public scene hot is the interaction between the viewers and the players in the scene. There is a power exchange in a public scene not just between the players but between the observers and the players as well. As I have said earlier, the power exchange is a big part of the thrill for me. The energy generated in a public scene can be overwhelming.

The biggest problem for people in a public space is balancing the knowledge that you are being observed with the interaction between Top and bottom. Often, though in the back of my mind I know I am being watched, I manage to tune out the crowd and mentally isolate myself with the bottom. I have had scenes in a dungeon where I was unaware of a large crowd watching until I was bringing the bottom "down" from the play. When I became aware of the people watching, it surprised me, even though I knew there were observers, I had no idea how many.

I guess a lot of this process goes back to the stage. Actors create an invisible fourth wall when they perform. They mentally tune out the audience in order to focus their energies on the other characters in a play. The theatre stage is different in that respect to the sideshow. Sideshow performers actively seek to engage the audience in their performance. Without the gawking spectators their acts have little significance. In the dungeon, players also create their own "fourth wall" yet if it were too effective, they might as well be playing in private. Playing in the dungeon or a public playspace means the players create a semitransparent "fourth wall", thick enough to avoid distractions, but thin enough to facilitate the power exchange with the observers.

Tuning In and Turning On and Shorting Out

About the time I was old enough to really enjoy music, my parents bought me a phonograph. For people who may not remember, or who are not old enough to even know, a phonograph or record player was a machine designed to play vinyl records. During my childhood these came in several varieties including, 78, 45 and 33.3rmp. (revolutions per minute)

My little record player was capable of only 78rmp and 45rpm, but that was all I needed. Most of my record collection was made up of bright yellow children's records and a few pop music 45's. I listened to music all the time, and my record player was my favorite toy. It had an amplifier built in and a tiny crappy speaker capable of only the most rudimentary sound reproduction, but I didn't care. I loved it.

I loved it for a long time and eventually it began to show signs of wear. What I didn't know at the time was that the tone arm had developed an electrical short. This combined with a failing capacitor ran voltage directly through the small metal arm. If I was touching the metal cabinet and the tone arm at the same time, the voltage ran directly through me! Luckily it wasn't enough to do any damage, but it was definitely enough to cause a shock.

If you have never experienced an electric shock, it is different from what you might expect. At low voltages and low amperages electric shocks cause mild tingling sensations. Increase the voltage and the tingling gets stronger. Increase the amperage and you can be seriously injured.

> **Big Warning** - *I am not an electrical engineer, so I will leave the details of this phenomenon to someone more qualified, but it is important to remember that thousands of people are killed each year by accidental electrocution. I strongly urge anyone considering experimenting with an old phonograph or any other electrical device to reconsider. Even a low voltage current running through your heart can kill you. Let me repeat, it can kill you!*

Now back to my story.

The shock I experienced was simply a strong tingling, it was enough to scare me at first and make me drop the tone arm right away. The problem was, it was not strong enough to hurt too much and I kind of liked it. Now, my favorite toy was not only a source of music, but of a sensation that I grew very fond of! I liked the electric shock and I liked the effect it had on my body even more. Not only did it tingle in my arm, but somewhere down between my legs! I was too young to get an erection, but something in my crotch really responded to the experience.

That memory stayed with me into adulthood and once I began experimenting in the realm of BDSM, I found that there were devices designed to administer that same feeling. These were not little red record players, but nifty gadgets designed by twisted engineers to deliver shocks at will. Once I discovered these gadgets, I knew I had to have more toys!

The reader will see a theme here, a fascination with toys that has never left me. I guess I am just a big kid at heart, because I love toys and the toys I get today are always more fun when they are shared. I like to think of my kink as something I can share with others. Especially willing bottoms who are eager to play with my toys!

Electrical toys are really good for administering precise doses of intense stimulation or pain. Since this book is all about pain, I just cannot get away without discussing electrical toys a bit.

There are lots and lots of electrical toys making their way to the kink marketplace. Many are very expensive and though they are tempting, I don't think the features outweigh the price. Personally, I like using my old standbys best. The following three electrical toys have served me well for many years and I expect they will do so in the future.

The Violet Wand

(Also know as the Master Violet Ray)

This is basically a Tesla Coil with a socket for attaching gas filled glass bulbs or electrodes. What this toy does is to discharge a static charge to anyone who is grounded and close enough to the electrode or bulb for a spark to jump. They are relatively safe and were used for years by quack doctors to do everything from cure colic in babies to grow hair on a bald man's head. They do neither of these yet are still used by some beauticians to "close the pores" after a facial.

The sparks from these gadgets can be quite spectacular and when using a metal electrode the effect can be very painful. This is what people expect electrocution to feel like, a sharp snap of a shock almost like being pricked by a pin. I have heard people say that the Violet Wand can leave sunburns due to the ultraviolet light the bulbs give off. From everything I have found, this is as bogus a claim as the one about growing hair. The bulbs give of no more ultra-violet light than a fluorescent light bulb. I have seen red spots on bottoms that are caused by the actual sparks, but these disappear after a day or two.

The Violet Wand is a great toy for demonstrations. It is showy and can be adjusted to be mild enough for a beginner or strong enough for the most experienced pain pig. I always use mine with a Ground Fault Interrupt (GFI Switch). This is a device that detects when a device connected to it has a potentially fatal malfunction. These are the same kind of plugs you see in bathrooms for shavers and hair dryers. They will automatically shut off via a circuit breaker if they detect a potentially hazardous short circuit. Without one of these there is a slight potential to have a health threatening electric shock and I try to always err on the side of caution.

Tens Unit

(Also available as Folsom Box®, Ero-Tek® or Electro-Stim®)

A TENS unit or Transcutaneous Electrical Nerve Stimulator is a real medical device used to relieve pain by stimulating the nerve ends without breaking the skin. It has shown to be effecting in cases of nerve damage and is prescribed in some cases for back pain, etc.

My first experience with a TENS was when a doctor gave me one for a problem with a muscle pull in my lower back. I am not a big fan of drug therapy for muscle pain, and he said that some of his patients had satisfactory results using a TENS unit.

The device itself is about the size of a portable cassette player and is powered by a 9 volt battery. It delivers the electric sensation through wires that attach to conductive pads. These pads are adhesive and contain an electrolytic adhesive to keep them on and to assure good contact for the current.

At low levels the feeling is somewhat like the tingling I got from my phonograph. It feels like there are little bugs crawling over your skin. At higher levels it becomes a real painful experience. There is still the tingling, but also a burning sensation. At very high levels it feels almost like someone has pricked you with a knife, or burned you with a cigarette. There should be no permanent damage with these toys, but the feeling they can deliver is profound.

In addition to the pads, various gadgets are available for adventurous players. These are mostly for the genitals, but there are attachments for other parts of the body as well. As a rule of thumb I never use a TENS unit above the waist. And never use it with anyone who has a pacemaker. The electrical impulses will disrupt the device and in turn disrupt their life! Not a pretty picture.

Among the toys are electric cock rings, clamps, electric bondage boards, probes and butt plugs. Used in various combinations these toys can offer almost endless fun. As long as the 9-volt batteries hold out. For the more intense player they even make models you can plug into the wall. For these as for any electrical device I recommend a Ground Fault Interrupt device between the TENS unit and the wall plug. More safety warnings!

Shock Rods, Cattle Prods, Stun Guns and more

For a brief and very intensely painful shock I like to use a cattle prod or Stun Gun. These are not the same Stun Guns used by police that shoot skin piercing electrodes on a wire, they are the hand held ones that are used for personal protection. The one I use is a hand held stun gun that delivers 80,000 volts with each shock. The secret is that these devices, like the violet wand have very low amperage. The shock delivered will not electrocute the person, but will cause muscle contractions that produce the painful effect.

Stun Guns are designed to immobilize a person or temporarily incapacitate them, because of this they deliver a much greater voltage shock than any other device. They can produce a temporary disorientation and this should be taken into consideration when playing with them.

Cattle prods are similar, but produce lower voltage shocks. These shocks sting and are designed to get cattle or people moving. The deliver a series of shocks in a rapid fire order and cause instantaneous pain. They are designed to use on livestock, and therefore use on people is discouraged by manufacturers. However, anyone old enough to remember the anti-war protests of the 1970's will recall police using these on protestors to get them to move during sit-ins. I can assure they encourage you to move!

In Context

So how do I use these gadgets in a scene? Glad you asked. I sometimes use my Folsom Box or TENS for CBT. This is not an acronym for "computer based training", it stands for "cock and ball torture." Since I covered the use of these devices in my previous book, *More Family Jewels*, I will only say that the sensations available using these machines is widely variable from mild to wild and depending on the positioning of the electrodes, the effect is pretty much pure pleasure. My favorite scene would involve a metal butt plug attached to one electrode and an electrically conductive cock ring attached to the other.

I use plenty of electro-lube, a substance that not only lubricates but provides sufficient electrolytic properties to get good electrical contact. This makes the cock ring/butt plug arrangement perfect for a male bottom. The electrical current seeks the shortest route between the electrodes, which in this case is the prostate gland. Let me assure you that a pulsating frequency from a TENS unit going through your prostate is a real party! The feeling is very much like having a long continuous orgasm. Your sphincter clenches and unclenches and your prostate throbs like crazy.

As you might be able to surmise, I have experienced this and can wholeheartedly endorse it as BIG FUN.

As for the other toys, I really like to combine them with other scenes. For me electrical toys can be the icing on the cake of a BDSM scene. For example, while doing a very elaborate piercing scene, I had my partner lay on a conductive pad. This was connected to a Violet Wand through a special attachment.

The scene was part of an initiation for Anna, a friend of mine. Her girl (and when I use this term I mean an adult who likes playing the role of a "girl") wanted to experience a piercing. Anna had asked me to do it since it was a specialty she was not skilled in. We arranged the scene to occur at a play party with friends present. Several of them watched as I carefully cleaned and prepared her girl for the scene. Once her skin was swabbed with a disinfectant scrub, I donned a pair of non-latex gloves and began the scene.

I pierced her chest above her breasts first, inserting a row of needles across her chest. Not long after the fourth or fifth needle was in, she was smiling and floating in a world of her own. The next needles I reserved for her breasts. I made circle around the nipples with the points facing the areola. The whole arrangement looked delightfully symmetrical, something I enjoy immensely.

Once the last needle was in her breasts, I removed my gloves and called over Anna and her friends. I showed her the cable leading from the pad her girl was lying on and picked up my Violet Wand. I turned the control up until it was making a audible buzzing sound, then I picked up a knife that I had in my toy bag. Holding the tip of the knife just a few inches from her girl's breasts I moved it slowly closer. As it reached a height of only about a quarter of an inch, a bright blue spark jumped from the tip to one of the needle points in her breast. She jumped at the shock. I slowly moved the knife around the ring of needles and sparks flew from the tip into the steel shafts of the needles. Some sparks even traveled from one point to another.

Since I was grounded, the knife in my hand was acting as a connection to ground the girl and complete the circuit of the static charge. Her friends soon got the idea and they used their fingers and knives and other metal toys to play with the charge themselves. Anna's girl was laughing from the tingling electrical sparks. In fact, the needles would serve to make the shocks less intense. Just as you can discharge static electricity in your body by touching a ground with a coin or a key, the same was true for the needles. The effect was as much visual as physical, since the room had the subdued lighting of a dungeon.

After a few minutes, her girl was almost out of breath she had been giggling so much. I turned the Violet Wand off and put on another pair of gloves. As I removed the needles and placed them in a sharps container, Anna leaned over and kissed her girl tenderly. She had been introduced to both piercing and electrical play and would be eager for more.

The Violet Wand and my other electrical toys are lots of fun, and when used cautiously they can be delightfully painful or pleasurable depending on my mood. I again caution anyone who wants to experience electrical play to find a knowledgeable player who knows the ins and outs of this kind of scene. Nothing can substitute for hands-on instruction.

Dancing With Pain

I keep going back to my earlier days to find instances when I got my first inklings of my kinky nature. It has been a surprising journey and one that validates a belief I have held for a long time. I think kinky folks, specifically people who are into SM are either born that way or develop the predilection very early in life.

I have an idea that we are all born somewhat pain-neutral. As children we experience pain as just another sensation unless it is extreme. If you are a diligent observer, you may see this in action. A child falls down, not a big fall, but just a little one and he catches himself with his hands. The hard slap of skin against pavement gets his mothers attention. Initially he just picks himself up and registers little distress, until his mother or father rushes to him and begins to program him to feel the sensation as pain.

How do they do this? Well, Mom or Dad sees little Hardy fall and they know he will be in pain, so they immediately start saying things like, "Oh did you hurt yourself? Aw, that must really hurt. Poor baby!"

They are programming little Hardy to interpret the sensation of his hands slapping against the pavement as painful, otherwise why all the sympathy? After their response it doesn't take long for little Hardy to start crying and often times much louder than you might expect from such a trivial fall.

I have no scientific proof of this, just my own experience, but I suspect there might be a few graduate students out there who might take this on for a project. I would love to know.

Among other childhood experiences, my perceptions of pain have been guided by art as well. I remember seeing a painting of Joan of Arc being burned at the stake. As she lifted her face upward, I saw in her eyes something I now recognize as not just a devoted stare into the eyes of God, but a look of ecstatic pain brought about as the flames leapt around her. That look has haunted me ever since, and I cannot locate that painting again. I would love to have a copy of it today, but so far my search has been fruitless.

Why is this important? Well, it really shows the dimensions pain can have on the mind and body. Pain can be a bad thing or a good thing depending on the circumstances, but it can also be something more. Pain can open a door to something much deeper in our minds and bodies. Remember the Yogi mystics that the sideshow talker mentioned? Well they do exist and they use pain as that gateway to a higher state of consciousness.

The best example of that I have witnessed was several years ago at a gathering of leatherfolk in Austin, Texas. It was one of those all weekend affairs with classes and seminars. The culmination was a big picnic far out in the hill country on a private ranch. That meant we could not only dine al fresco, but would be able to have BDSM play outside as well, a rare occurrence unless you have lots of land and few neighbors.

At the picnic, Peter, a fellow Top and good friend of mine asked me to help him in a scene. He had found a willing and very hunky participant named Randy who had agreed to the scene. What he proposed doing was a specialty of his and I had seen him do it before, but actually being part of it made the whole scene much better.

Peter had developed a version of the "Ball Dance" ritual. This is derived from a Southeast Asian spiritual practice that involves fruit being attached to the body by metal hooks or sewn to the body with thread. Once the participants are festooned with dozens of limes, oranges, lemons and other fruit they begin spinning and dancing. Their fervor is driven by a spiritual as well as physical engine that blurs the lines between what is pain and what is pleasure. In a transcendent dance of ecstasy they spin faster and faster until the fruit flies from their bodies. In the process the hooks also pull out and often there is a good deal of blood. As a way to eliminate the blood, and make the experience less invasive, Peter put his own twist on it.

He took 3 or 4 ounce fishing weights, about the size of golf balls and attached them to leather cords about 2 feet long. At the ends of the cords he fastened small alligator clamps. These are the kind of clamps you find at Radio Shack for use in electronic testing. The tiny clamps have teeth to help them grip. Peter takes several dozen of these and attaches them to the skin of his play partner in a pattern that allows the weight to hang and swing freely. Attachment points vary, but mostly along the arms and chest and abdomen.

What makes this scene so special is the manner in which Peter does it. He performs it as a ritual, not just an SM scene. The day I helped him, he had brought a portable CD player and had Native American tribal music on hand. The beat of the drums and the wistful flute helped set the stage for the scene.

Randy took off his clothes while Peter and I prepared by carefully laid out all the weights and clamps in neat rows on a bench. Once we were set, Peter stood before Randy and looked deep into his eyes. Neither of them spoke, but I could see as Peter brought his hands to Randy's shoulders that they were connecting in a deep way. Peter let his fingers trail down the sides of Randy's arms then continues down his hips and legs to the ground. It was as though he was brushing away any negative energy that might be left in Randy's body.

He then lifted Randy's arms until they were stretched out parallel to the ground. Looking over his shoulder he nodded to the bench and I picked up one of the leather cords with weight and clips attached. As I handed it to him his gaze had returned to Randy and he slowly moved to his outstretched arm. There he attached one clip to the flesh of his forearm and the other to the skin near his elbow. The weight swung gently as he attached the clips. Randy continued to stare into Peter's eyes, making only the slightest grimace as Peter applied the clips.

Peter worked slowly and methodically, watching Randy's body language carefully. He looks for signs that Randy had reached his limit of what he could take. As I handed him the weights, I saw Randy slowly transform from just a hunky naked man into what I would call a sacred being. He was covered with two dozen of the weights, their leather thongs creating a symmetrical graphic pattern across his body.

As Peter hung the last of the weights from the skin of Randy's chest he turned to me and motioned for me to move behind Randy. I would act like a "spotter" should Randy loose his balance, but also as an active participant in the scene.

Peter placed his fingers under Randy's outstretched arms and gently began guiding him in slow sweeping movements. Soon Randy began moving on his own, wrapped in the haunting flute music and soaring from the energy being released. Peter and I moved with him, surrounding him in a loosely defined circle with our outstretched arms.

Randy's eyes closed and he began to moan in a low rumbling voice. His movements changed from a slow swaying, to a gentle turning dance. Each gesture and movement made the weights swing and sway from his body. The movement also made the alligator clips pull and tug with the motion of the weights.

Soon all three of us were moving together. We were dancing with Randy as he danced in the pain and ecstasy of the clips and weights. His skin was on fire with the sensations and each movement carried with it waves of pain and pleasure. Randy was in an almost trance like state, and the energy he was giving off was palpable. The world vanished and only Peter, Randy and I remained. We moved and swayed with the music in a dance choreographed only by the sensations Randy was feeling.

After almost 20 minutes Peter approached Randy and slowed his movements. He held his face in his hands and looked into Randy's eyes. After whispering a few words of affection, Peter motioned to me to move closer. I held Randy as Peter began removing the clips from his skin.

By now, Randy was deep into an endorphin high and was still riding the strains of the music. As Peter gently removed each clip, they left behind teeth marks, like a tiny alligator had bitten Randy's skin. Amazingly, no skin was broken, though the area surrounding the marks was red and swollen from the trauma.

Randy began to slump in my arms as Peter removed the last of the clips. He then moved close and we both embraced Randy between us. For a few minutes, we just remained in the three-way hug. We were feeling the energy flowing from Randy and experiencing the profound connection that we had made.

After a few minutes, we parted and Peter helped Randy sit down. I brought him some water and he slowly become fully conscious again. Though he had been through an excruciatingly painful ritual, he was smiling from ear to ear. Randy was giddy from the natural opiates still coursing through his body, but he was also very happy to have been part of the ritual. What happened between Peter and Randy was beyond mere communication, it was a spiritual bonding made more profound by the ritual aspects of the scene. By conducting it that way, Peter had initiated Randy into his close circle of friends. He had shared a very intimate moment and had given Randy an amazing experience. I, too, shared that moment. It was a bonding experience for all three of us.

Since that day, I have made my own set of weights for the ball dance. I put my own personal twist on it and have used it several times in scenes. It is something that I will use only on special people, people with whom I feel a deep connection. The ritual aspects of it are part of what makes this activity so intense, both physically and emotionally. Every time I have done the "ball dance" with a friend, it has bonded us deeper in our friendship.

Just as painful rituals were used by other cultures to initiate individuals into a group, this ritual and others like it are our initiations. In this case, we unlearn some of the attitudes we were taught about pain from our childhood. We come to accept ritual pain as not only a rite of passage, but also a desirable thing that can serve as an intimate bond between people. SM rituals give us a chance to move beyond the mere acts of play and into the realm of deeper communication and spiritual enlightenment.

A Moth to the Flame

Birthdays are always memorable events for kids. They become a memory montage of silly paper hats, brightly colored punch, pointless games and cake, lots of cake. Interspersed with those images are a few others like smacking a piñata with an old broom handle and an explosion of candy and toys, and the occasional bout of over-full stomach resulting in a gastric piñata of sorts. But I digress.

The mandatory birthday cake was always the grand finale of these parties, and with it came the candles. At first I could never blow these things out, but as I grew older and bigger my lung capacity made it less of a challenge. After blowing out the candles, the cake was a smoldering smudge pot from the still glowing wicks. My mother would pinch each one out and quickly pluck the spent candles from the cake.

One year, I decided to help out, and I pinched out a candle. What I failed to notice was that mom had pinched only the wick. I pinched the still molten wax, and the candle stuck fast to my finger. After a few moments of shock at the sudden heat that would not let go of my finger, I shook the candle off. Like most of my early experiences, this one made me think. The wax was hot, but not so hot that it would raise a blister on my finger. It was an interesting sensation, and one that I would explore later in life.

I suspect it was that early experience with the birthday candles that sparked my interest in fire. As I grew older, I was continually drawn to flames and any excuse to light them. Before you get the wrong idea, I wasn't a pyromaniac. I understood the potential danger in fire, a point that was driven home to me every Christmas.

We always had a real Christmas tree. My mom loved the smell and just wouldn't be caught with a fake one in the house. We put our tree up after Thanksgiving and by New Years Eve it was beginning to lose its needles. My father liked to take our old trees and burn them in the fireplace. We burned the tree in small bundles, since the dry pine almost exploded when lit in the fireplace. That violent fire made me very aware of how dangerous flames could be. I got a little close and got singed on more than one occasion.

Still a healthy respect for fire didn't prevent me from continuing to experiment with it. More succinctly with candles. I managed to snag a couple of dozen from various sources including birthday candles, old Hanukkah candles and an occasional full sized candle from the dinner table. (Hanukkah candles because my father was Jewish and my mother was Christian. She later converted but both she and my dad loved the Christmas trees. Go figure?)

The thing I really enjoyed was dripping the wax from the candles and watching how it built up in interesting patterns on my skin. It was not uncommon to have a melted glob of colored wax on the back of my hand by the end of my experiment. That feeling and experience served me very well later in life. Today, I love playing with hot wax and candles in the dungeon.

One of the most interesting things to me about wax is the ability to focus specific sensations in exact spots. As you might have gathered by now, I like delivering pain with precision. Call it what you will, the ability to control the amount and specifics of pain really makes it valuable as a plaything. Sloppy pain delivery is just brutality, but doing it in a precise manner is artistry, and heaven knows as a gay man I love the idea of making art.

I even incorporated a candle scene in a short film I directed back in 1995 called *Leather*. The Top in my film was a close friend who not only knew what he was doing, he was good looking, a nice combination. We filmed the scene in a totally dark studio with only a single soft light suspended above the scene and the light from the candles. The effect was stunning and the scene came across as very hot.

My friend who was Topping in the scene was duplicating the technique I use in the dungeon. He had watched me do a wax scene several times and he reproduced it admirably.

My scene starts with the bottom lying naked on his back. I covered the play area in a piece of black plastic, the same kind used by painters and contractors. I had in my supplies 8-10 black candles. I got these at a local herb & witchcraft shop. They are about the size of the emergency candles you can obtain from the hardware store, but they are in various colors for "spells". The shop owner eyed me suspiciously since I bought a bag full of only black candles whenever I visited his shop.

I wear black leather gloves when I play these kinds of scenes. I like the feel of the leather, and it looks sexy, and that's reason enough. I also carry a large Bowie knife. This is a long knife with an 8" blade. It's an imposing knife, and being faced with it can raise the adrenaline level very rapidly.

I begin the scene by lighting a single candle and letting it burn until melted wax begins to pool around the wick. Once enough is built up, I begin dripping it onto the bottom. I vary the height of the drips, and thus vary the sensation of the hot wax. Higher, the wax cools during its fall and is less painful. Lower it is hotter and more painful.

I like using black candles for several reasons. First, the drops are easier to see if playing with someone with lighter skin. Second, they look mysterious. Black is color often associated with evil or dark side activities and I find the association puts a subtle edge on the scene. Pink candles or other "happy" colors just wouldn't have the same effect.

I drip a pattern on the bottom's skin, sometime making concentric circles, other times random patterns. I avoid the nipples at first and save them for later in the scene. The patterns also let the bottom anticipate where the next sensation will occur. It is somewhat comforting and as you will see a deception on my part.

Once I have completed about half of the pattern, I light a second candle. Using one candle in each hand I continue making patterns with the drops of hot wax. The additional candle adds to the experience for the bottom, who has by now become used to the sensations. The drips now happen twice as fast which will increase the adrenaline and endorphins for the bottom. With the second candle I do some concentration on the nipples, coating them simultaneously with wax droplets.

I then add a third and fourth candle, holding two in each hand between my fingers much in the way I would hold a cigar. The drips are now much faster and the patterns grow larger. The effect on the bottom is one of a slight confusion, since they no longer really can anticipate where the next drops are going to fall.

I then transfer all four candles to my right hand, holding one between each finger I can now shake my hand slightly and create a rain of drops anywhere I choose. While I am doing this, I pick up four more candles and arrange then in my left hand in the same way as the first four. I light them using the already lit ones in my right hand. Now I begin a fully fledged rain of hot wax on the bottoms skin. They are suitably charged with endorphins to accept this pain and the randomness of the drops removes any anticipation from their mind. They tell me it was like floating in a shower of fire.

Once their skin is evenly splattered with the black wax and I feel they have reached their limit for the scene, I blow the candles out. Setting them down I allow the bottom to enjoy the sensation of the rain of wax stopping. The last of the warmth from the drops fades and they return to a somewhat normal state. Sometimes I run my fingers over the splattered wax patterns giving the bottom another sensation to process, albeit a much more sensual one.

Once I have let them relax a bit I pick up my knife. I like to make sure they see it and understand that they must remain very still to avoid injury. Immediately their adrenaline level spikes again. There is a natural reaction to a knife that is learned in early childhood. Knives are dangerous and sharp. And in this case I have heightened that effect by reminding them of the danger.

Note for Tops only:

I like to play safely, and some say I am overly cautious, but I find I rarely get into trouble that way. The bowie knife I use in this scene is specially prepared. It looks and even feels sharp at first; however I have dulled the blade using a piece of emery paper. This extremely fine-grain abrasive takes the edge off the blade without making it appear dull. With enough force I could chop something with the knife, but I get it to a point where it is dull enough to be safely dragged across the skin without cutting. I then polish the blade to remove any scratches the dulling process might have left.

This sounds like a lot of work, but it really takes only an hour or so to do a good job, and the knife can be used over and over without worrying about having to do it again.

I take the knife and lay the blade flat against the bottom's skin. I slowly scrape it across their skin, peeling the wax up as the edge presses against them. The action resembles shaving and feels like you are peeling their skin away. It is not painful, but very sensual and intensely erotic for most bottoms.

I discard the peeled wax with each stroke, keeping the blade clean assures that the shaving sensation will be consistent. I save peeling the wax from the nipples for last, since it focuses attention on what for most people is an erogenous zone.

After the scene, I remain with the bottom, usually holding them in my arms or on my lap to allow them to come down from the natural "high" they have experienced. It is a bonding moment for us and also allows me to return to a less focused and intense mindset.

Wax play can be done in a multitude of ways. Some Tops prefer to use crock pots to melt large quantities of wax and apply it with a brush or ladle, others use votive candles and pour wax in patterns on the skin. I even have a friend who uses votive candles to turn the bottom into a candelabrum. It is a very beautiful and impressive scene.

For safety reasons, I always keep a fire extinguisher handy in my toy bag and a large towel which can be used to snuff flames should they get out of control. Anytime you play with fire, there is a chance of getting burned, so again safety is a prime concern.

I use the cheapest candles I can find. Most of these are made with low quality Paraffin and have a melting pint of around 133° F. Since the wax cools some as it is dripped burns are not a problem. I have heard people say that Beeswax is dangerous because it has a much higher melting point, however the melting point for beeswax is only 140° and as such it does not seem to be that much of a problem. Now remember I am not a physicist, so take these figures with a little skepticism and experiment on yourself to make sure. Afraid to try it on yourself? Then you have no business trying it on someone else!

More Fireworks

I was a shy child. Though many of my friends would deny it, I am still painfully shy; I have just learned to cope with it. Part of learning to cope with that shyness came from my hobby as a youngster. I did magic.

Magic had a tremendous appeal to a shy kid like me. It gave me something that other kids and for that matter adults didn't have, a secret. Now growing up as a gay kid, I had another secret that I kept pretty well hidden until my high school years, but magic was different. The secrets a magician holds have power, power to amaze people and power to entertain. As just an ordinary kid, I had no special attributes that would call attention to me, but as a magician I was very special.

I wasn't a particularly good magician, but I enjoyed it and magic gave me those coping tools to deal with my shyness. I learned how to speak clearly and to hold a groups attention. I learned how to direct people's attention to whatever action or subject I wanted. This misdirection is critical for a magician, and as I have learned, for a Top as well.

Aside from the people skills, Magic brought me into contact with all kinds of new gadgets and apparatus. One of the things I fell in love with was being able to conjure fire at my command. Remember that story about the candles? Well my fascination with fire was deepened with my activities as a magician. I am not exposing a big secret when I tell you about a little item that fascinated me in the magic shop. I apologize in advance to any brother or sister magicians who may be miffed by this, but since it is such common knowledge I don't think it will hurt,

I am talking about "flash cotton". Actually known as nitrocellulose, flash cotton is more commonly known as "gun cotton". It has been around for hundreds of years and was used to ignite cannons and pistols in the days before self contained bullets. It is an ephemeral stuff, made by soaking cotton in nitric and sulfuric acid. It's not the kind of stuff you make at home. Consider that a warning!

I learned how dangerous making Flash Cotton was when a specialty manufacturer, who made small quantities of the stuff in his basement, had an accident. It only takes one accident with explosives, and in his case it blew him through a brick wall, much like a cartoon explosion. The unfunny part was that he was dead.

This story has always stayed with me to remind me of the potential danger of any pyrotechnics or fire. As I have said before I try to be extra cautious in my play.

The nifty thing about Flash Cotton is the way it burns. Because the fibers have been degraded and infused with a nitrate, they combust rapidly and burn almost without any residue. The temperature is not as hot as some fires, burning a bright yellow. The speed at which it burns makes it great for a magician who wants a quick bright flash to misdirect an audience. Additionally, the fast burn makes it something that can be ignited while resting on a magician's hand without leaving a burn. As long as the skin is below the flame, burns are almost impossible. Remember that high school physics class? Heat rises, therefore skin below the flame is relatively safe. Above the flame, and you got yourself a third or second degree burn! Consider that another warning.

Today, I still do a little magic, but my main interest lies in the dungeon, and there I perform a very different kind of magic. That is not to say I don't use some of the tricks I learned as a junior magician in my play. I do.

Flash Cotton is one of my favorite toys for inducing very controlled pain and giving a bottom a really intense "rush". Again I emphasize

I never use this stuff where the flame will rise and burn skin above it. This means no use under balls, penis, and breasts or between legs of a standing person.

I prefer doing these kinds of scenes with the bottom lying down. I play on their back or front depending on the preferences of the bottom and of course me. This way, there is little chance of accidental burns and I have a less limited space in which to play.

Flash cotton is easily obtainable at a local magic shop; before using it, you have to dry it out. It is shipped and sold moistened in water. This retards the burning and makes it safe to ship. I dry out a package at a time, leaving any packets I have stored still wet for safety. Needless to say, let it air-dry. Don't use a blow dryer or worse an open flame to try to dry it. You will end up with a potentially disastrous fire on your hands, maybe literally!

I prepare for the scene by spinning the cotton fibers into thin threads. These are about the size of kite string and are rolled between the fingers and drawn out to a uniform thickness. The resulting threads look a little like thin yarn. I test burn a couple to see if they are sufficiently tight to burn fast and not too thick to reduce potential accidental skin burns.

As the scene begins, I like to take a few minutes to touch the bottom and let him or her feel my hands moving over their skin. It heightens the sensitivity of their skin and also lets us connect before the scene intensifies. I like to stay in touch physically with a bottom when I play. It gives them reassurance and a grounding that helps them process the sensations. Additionally, abruptly withdrawing touch or sensation from a bottom can induce an abandonment reaction that can color the overall impression of the scene.

Once I feel they are ready, I begin laying a few short strips of the Flash Cotton on his or her body. I try to stay away from very sensitive areas with the first few strips to allow the bottom to adjust to the new sensation. If they have never played with Flash Cotton before, it is not extremely painful, but the element of fire and heat gets the body's chemical factory going really fast.

After I have laid out a few short strips, about 12 inches in length, I ignite them one by one using a cigar if the dungeon permits smoking. If not, I sometimes use a candle or a small gadget found in the magic shop which is used to create seemingly magical bursts of flame from the magician's hand.

The latter device is particularly effective if the bottom doesn't know about it. It allows you to ignite the flash cotton with only the force of your will in their minds. Remember bottoms are vulnerable, and though I often use that vulnerability for harmless tricks, I do not betray their trust or try to control them by deception.

One other way I have ignited flash cotton is with a violet wand. The spark thrown from one of the metal probes that come with some Violet Wand setups is sufficient to start the cotton burning. Again it's almost magical and it adds another dimension of pain to the scene.

The flash cotton strings will burn very rapidly with a bright yellow flame. They smell a little like burned hair, and that odor, though offensive to some actually may heighten the excitement for some bottoms. It's a very distinctive odor and most people will react to it with a bit of fear or apprehension. That can put a really fun "edge" on a scene. The bottom knows you are trust worthy, but the fear reaction plants a small seed of doubt that adds to the natural adrenaline effect.

I then proceed to longer strips, some winding around areas of the body like breasts or pubic areas. The rapid movement of the flame sends a directed sensation toward the end of the strip, so it is not uncommon for a strip that runs toward an erogenous zone to trigger a quick erogenous response. One woman I played with had a spontaneous orgasm with a well directed strip of flash cotton that ended about an inch from her clitoris. It was a surprise for both of us!

I will continue a flash cotton scene until the bottom is suitably aroused. What that means is that they are so stimulated from the heat and flames that to go further would be superfluous. I have also used flash cotton scenes as preludes for other play, especially if it will involve pain, since the flash cotton will prime the endorphin pump with very little effort.

I have also used flash cotton in conjunction with another scene. One of my favorites is to end a clothespin scene with a zipper across the bottom's chest. I secretly add a strip of flash cotton into the clothespins so that it is held away from the body about 2 inches. Right before I pull the zipper off, I ignite the flash cotton with my magician's gadget and the combination of the pain from the zipper and the surprise of the flash cotton give the bottom a real treat. It's also showy and great for demos and lectures. I guess that magician's training never goes away!

Pins & Needles

About the time I started the fourth grade, my body decided it didn't like Texas. More specifically it decided it didn't like some of the plants and animals of Texas. I began to develop allergies and they manifest themselves in the form of asthma. The wheezing of asthma is annoying, but it is not the real problem. The sounds come from the various tubes and pockets in your lungs swelling. As the swell, they whistle against each other like the reeds in a clarinet. Once they are sufficiently swollen there is a different problem, oxygen.

I guess this is why I have never been particularly fond of breath play; I experienced it non-consensually for many years as a child and adolescent. The effects of a severe asthma attack make taking as much as a tablespoon full of air almost impossible. Without help, you can pass out, get brain damage, or worse, die. Luckily I had a doctor for a father. Though he wasn't an MD he did work at a hospital and we always had great medical care. In the emergency room, they gave me an inhaler with some kind of bronchodilator in it and a couple of shots of ACTH, adrenaline to open up my passages. What a rush!

Unless you have experienced the panic and agony of an asthma attack you would not have much of an idea what taking a full breath is like afterward. You get lightheaded, feel an overall giddiness and promptly hyperventilate. Add to that the endorphins and other bodily emergency chemicals coursing through your veins and you have a recipe for one higher-than-a-kite kid.

In order to mitigate the problem, my parents sent me to an allergy specialist to get tested for allergens. The test may have changed since then, but at the time it consisted of having small circles drawn on your forearms and various possible allergens applied to the skin with a small lancet or blade. The skin is scratched lightly to make sure some of the allergen gets under the surface.

Additionally, they marked off one hundred spots on my back and proceeded to give me tinny injections under the skin of additional allergens. Each injection was done using a very fine insulin needle, so the pain was minimal. Well it would have been minimal if it had only been one or two sticks; one hundred is a different story.

The scratches on my arms didn't seem too bad, and I know now that this mild trauma got my body's pain defenses going pretty quickly. The injections in my back were a different story. They hurt, at least the first six or seven did. After that I really had no problem. By the time they had finished the injections I was almost giggling. I was in a euphoric state that made me quite talkative and charming, at least that was what I thought at the time.

I had to wait a couple of hours for the allergens to do their dirty work and for the doctor to read the test. While I waited, I simply coasted on the endorphin high as long as I could. By the time the doctor got to me I had started to itch. The spots where I had been scratched or injected had begun to get red, and the ones that got the reddest were the culprits. Turns out I was allergic to almost everything including camel hair and every pollen known to man.

The doctor gave my mother a check list of what I should avoid and sent me on my way with a pocket full of inhalers and several bottles of pills.

Besides learning what I was allergic to, I also learned how quickly the body reacts to anything invasive. A needle stick is about as invasive as you can get with the exception of a scalpel, knife or bullet. This knowledge would serve me well in my later, kinky life.

Playing with needles is not nearly as dangerous as it seems, if you take reasonable precautions and use only sterile single use needles. Additionally you need to know what and where you can pierce and where you can't. Rather than give a dry step-by-step of temporary piercing, I think a story of a very memorable scene would be better.

As with most of these stories, I have a stern warning. Do not attempt a temporary piercing scene without having someone who is experienced teach you. Hands-on instruction is the only way to really learn this kind of play. Especially with all the blood borne pathogens out there these days, a piercing scene is edge play in most people's books. Because of that, you need to know what you are doing to avoid harming the bottom and yourself. People in the health care field are infected with blood-borne pathogens on a regular basis because they failed to take proper precautions, had an accident or just got careless. All it takes is a single needle stick with a contaminated needle to catch a life-threatening disease. HIV is most often transmitted to health-care workers through needle sticks, and these are people who do the sticking for a living. That fact alone should be sobering, but there are lots more nasty new diseases going around and new ones pop up regularly, so consider yourself warned.

It was Jean's birthday and as a special treat, her Domme had asked me to help out with her gift. Jean had wanted to do a piercing scene and her Domme was going to oblige with a doozie. She contacted me several weeks before the event to make sure I could be present. Additionally, I arranged to have all the supplies we needed at hand to do the scene. I also had the keys to the dungeon where the piercing and the party following were to take place. Having those keys got me invited to a lot of great parties!

Prior to the event, I acquired a couple of boxes of sterile, single-use disposable needles. For this event I chose 20 gage needles, 1.5 inches in length. These are strong enough to use and safely avoid any bending or breaking, but not so large that they will cause a lot of bleeding. Blood! Yup, when you break the skin you tend to bleed. Now this isn't the kind of bleeding that you see from an opened vein, but a few drops are unavoidable.

Because of the presence of blood, I made sure we had a supply of sterile latex-free surgical gloves on hand (pun intended). These are the purple gloves you see the police use. They are non-latex to avoid any problems with latex allergies. Some people do not even know they have this allergy, so why take chances? Additionally, I had a bottle of a surgical skin scrub preparation, the kind without iodine, and a fresh package of sterile gauze.

If this sounds like I was preparing for surgery, it is somewhat similar, but nowhere near as complex. We had a medical exam table in the dungeon, but for this event we wanted something more interesting. Our dungeon had a table that was suspended from chains. This table was great for bondage or other scenes where the bottom could "float" after being restrained. The gentle swaying motion of the table gave a very lighter-than-air feeling to it and it was a fun place for a scene. For our scene we had covered the table in a disposable plastic sheet just in case there was any blood that couldn't be absorbed by the gauze sponges.

I had a clean stainless steel table positioned nearby, the kind used in actual surgery, that we had picked up at a hospital supply store clearance sale. I covered it with several layers of clean paper towels to act as a work surface and topped it with a fresh "sharps" container. These red plastic jugs are the best way to contain and dispose of needles, scalpel blades and in a clinic they also are used for syringes. They are made of a tough plastic that keeps the sharp contaminated needles contained and safely away from possible accidents. They have tops that seal once they are full and they can be disposed of safely later.

An additional item I had ready was a box of birthday candles, but more about those later.

Jean and her friends arrived after a dinner party and we all spent some time socializing and swapping stories until everyone had arrived. Once all the guests were safely inside, I locked the door and we adjourned to the play area of the dungeon. Our dungeon was really a small warehouse that was divided into a showroom/office area in the front and a large open space in the back. We had painted the walls with a weathered stone motif and added special lighting to accentuate the specific play areas. St Andrew's Crosses, racks, cages, and platforms were arranged around the space to provide good access for the people involved in a scene and plenty of room for spectators. We had installed a pretty nice sound system as well to provide the appropriate music. For tonight's scene, we were the only people using the space and the music was a specially mixed tape of deep trance/ tribal drumming songs.

Jean's Domme whispered to Jean that is was time for her present, and guided her toward the suspended table. Jean carefully removed her leather vest and shirt, folding them neatly and placing them on a chair. She sat on the table and her Domme approached her. Placing her hands on Jean's shoulders she looked into Jean's eyes and smiled. "You are a very special boi to me, and because you are so special, I have arranged this scene for your birthday."

Jean nodded and replied in a respectful tone," Thank you Mistress, I am sure I will enjoy it and I will enjoy the pleasure it brings to you as well."

Her Domme smiled and gently guided Jean back onto the table. As she lay there she looked up at me and gave me a hint of a smile. Jean and I were close friends and this was a special scene for me as well. To be asked to participate in an SM scene by another Top, especially when it is to join him or her in playing with their significant other is a great honor. It is one that I never take lightly and it really makes the scene special for me as well.

I opened a package of sterile gloves by ripping open the top, then pulled out the inner paper wrapper and laid it on the table. The wrapper is designed to be opened without touching the gloves themselves, keeping their surface sterile before use. Unfolding the paper I offered them to Jean's Domme. She slid the fingers of her right hand into the sleeve of the first glove and pulled it on holding the wrist of the glove by the cuff. By taking care to do it this way, her fingers never touched the outer surface of the glove, keeping it sterile. Then she picked up the second glove by sliding the fingers of her gloved right hand under the cuff of the second glove and lifted it enough to insert her left hand. She pulled the glove down over her fingers holding the cuff and then rolled the cuff down over her wrist. This technique is used by nurses and surgeons in the operating room to avoid contaminating the sterility of the surgical gloves. I opened the second package of gloves and donned them in the same manner.

One of our friends also slipped on a pair of gloves and began laying out the needles we would use for the scene. This night we were going to use a whole box, one hundred. It would be a very special scene indeed. We used the kind of disposable needles that are contained in a small plastic tube. These are capped and sealed to preserve their sterility. The seal makes a snapping sound once broken, and no snap, it means the needle may not be sterile. These go by various brand names but the ones we were using were called Monoject©.

We began by preparing Jean's skin. Since we were going to put needles in her arms, chest and legs, we needed to clean the skin so there would be less chance of an infection in one of the puncture points. We used the kind of antibacterial scrub use in modern surgery and applied it with sterile gauze pads, referred to as sponges in the medical community.

Using a circular motion working from the center of the area out we scrubbed her skin, changing sponges between applications and doing our best not to contaminate the area.

In reality, practicing sterile technique was impossible in the setting of a dungeon. First of all, the place is not all that clean. Though we regularly mopped the floors and cleaned all the surfaces with disinfectant, it was still just a warehouse, not an operating room. The exercise of sterile style technique was as much a ritual as it was a precaution. Still we would be making sure we did our best to prevent any unanticipated problems.

Once Jean's Domme and I finished cleaning her, we put on a fresh pair of gloves and began. Our assistant handed us each a needle, holding the tube that surrounded the point of the needle and letting us grasp it by the hub, the part that would normally attach to a syringe.

We worked in unison and slowly and deliberately matched our movements so the experience would be happening on both sides of Jean's body at once. Working in time to the slow trance-like beat, we placed the first needles into her upper chest. We carefully pinched a small fold of skin and slid the needle through it and back out the other side. We made sure the points faced inward to minimize any risk of accidently sticking ourselves by brushing up against them.

Jean flinched and then let out a whimper as the first two needles pierced her flesh. We waited for her to process the sensation and then took two more needles. These went in about a half an inch below the first, parallel to the needle already in place. Again Jean let out a whimper, but I saw a slight smile start to appear on her face.

After we had added about ten or twenty more needles to the rows, we began working on Jean's arms. We carefully inserted a row of needles up her forearms, placing them just under the skin perpendicular to her arm. This ladder of needles went from her wrist to her shoulder. We carefully avoided hitting any veins to prevent profuse bleeding.

After a brief pause, we started on her legs. We only worked with the thighs, where the skin was sufficiently pliable, creating more needle ladders all the way up to her crotch.

Her Domme checked in with her often and made sure she was still in the right "head-space" to continue. Jean was having trouble containing her joy. She was rushing on endorphins as well as the happiness of the special occasion.

Finally we came to her breasts. We had about 20 needles each and began inserting these in a circle around the sides of her areolas. The points faced inward so that when either of us pressed on her nipples, the points grazed her areola; not piercing, but still very stimulating!

As the last few needles completed the circle, we still had 5 needles each left. Jean's Domme had some medical training and knew quite a bit about anatomy. She had given injections to relatives in critical health care situations and knew where you could safely insert a long needle without hitting anything critical. The top of the thighs work very well for this kind of thing, and though I would never suggest anyone try this without proper instruction, they make a great place for needle play. Much to Jean's surprise, the needles we pierced her with here went in straight into the muscle of the thigh. This is a very different sensation that the subcutaneous piercings we had been doing.

Jean sat up a bit to watch with wonder and a little fear as we pushed the full length of the needles into her thighs. Once the last needle was in, her Domme smiled and said to her, "just one more finishing touch for your birthday gift."

Our assistant handed us each five birthday candles and we placed them into the aluminum hubs of the needles we had just placed in Jean's thighs. They fit perfectly making her legs look like a birthday cake. I pulled out my lighter and lit the candles as all three of us sang the birthday song to her.

OK, it's really a twisted scene, but it was perfect for Jean and she was giggling as she tried to blow the candles out without pricking herself on the hundred needles that studded her body. Her Domme took a couple of photographs of Jean glistening with needles for souvenirs, and then we started to remove the needles.

Again we worked in tandem so the scene would have symmetry both in its look and in the sensations Jean was receiving. As we withdrew the needles, we placed them into the sharps containers immediately. I never try to recap a used needle. Most accidental needle sticks in the medical field come from trying to recap needles, so it's just safer and easier to put them directly in the sharps containers.

Occasionally we paused to wipe up a little blood, but in general, Jean didn't bleed much. Every scene is different, and some people bleed more than others. People on blood thinners and those who have just taken aspirin are more susceptible to bleeding, and that is something to consider before doing a piercing scene.

The needles in her legs were the last to be removed. Because they went straight in. they bled very little, much like the site of an injection. As the last needle came out, Jean's Domme leaned down and kissed her boi with a deep passionate kiss.

I always love seeing the kind of genuine affection between players in a scene, and this one would be in my memory for a long time. Years later, Jean still has the photos of the scene and fondly remembers that night. I feel privileged to have been a part of it.

I Got Rhythm

My first exposure to music making as a child was listening to my mother play the piano. She was not a great pianist, but she sincerely loved the act of playing and loved her piano. As I grew older she let me sit by her as she practiced, and soon I was allowed to bang on the keys a little myself.

At first I got nothing but a rhythmic cacophony from the instrument. Little hands slapping keys at random rarely produce a sweet melody. In later life I came to appreciate Schoenberg's atonal works and other less traditional music, but as a child I longed to make melody and rhythm. Ten years of piano lessons made that dream a reality, though reading music has always been a struggle. Seems people with Dyslexia have a problem with musical notation.

I still play the keyboard, and thanks to the computer I can write music without the confusion of the musical staff. Other than the piano, I was always attracted to drums. I think they are the most basic instrument we have and they touch something primal in all of us. In preschool, everyone has played in a rhythm-band and the joy of beating out a tempo together with drums, shakers and tambourines is a delightful experience. That urge to beat the drum has never left me.

I briefly toyed with drumming as an adult. My efforts gave me a new respect for percussionists. I was awful, especially at keeping the beat. However, I really enjoyed it.

Eventually, apartment living brought an end to my flirtation with drumming. Seems not everyone you live next to appreciates music.

Given my love of rhythm and music it is hardly a surprise that I found a way to bring that passion into the dungeon. When I was part owner of a public playspace here in Dallas, I took it upon myself to put together a library of background music. I am a big fan of trance/dance and other electronic as well as the more tribal beats of some new age artists. From my personal music collection and that of my friends I managed to amass a nice selection of CDs for our dungeon. Since we didn't have a DJ working during parties, though I put together a sound system that would allow this, we mainly relied on a multi-disk changer to provide the music flow.

What I noticed during our parties was the effects the music had on the participants. There were certain songs that rally ramped up the energy level of the party. During my scenes, I too found that certain music was much more appealing for certain scenes than others. Specifically, impact play such as flogging, spanking or rough body play really was affected by the beat and character of the music.

Today, I find I incorporate that rhythm into my play. I began by just keeping the beat to whatever music was playing in the dungeon or playroom at the time. Spanking a nice bare butt, bent over you knee in time to a good beat is lots of fun. However, I soon found that though I might be having fun, sometimes the bottom was getting too much too fast.

Part of being a good Top is learning how to bring your bottom to a peak experience, not just brutalize them. With practice, I learned to utilize the rhythms of the music as a way of enhancing the scene for the bottom as well. I have found this especially useful in direct hand to body contact scenes. What might be called rough body play can become a rhythmic ritualized beating that transcends a simple SM scene.

I began to explore the spiritual connection of drumming, rhythm and

SM and learned some interesting things. Now stay with me because I am going to get a little "new age" on you.

Drumming really connects with my inner child. It allows me to lose myself in the rhythm and see things with new eyes. Drumming can be a form of meditation for me, synchronizing the left and the right brain hemispheres. The two brain hemispheres usually issue different wave frequencies but drumming utilizes both so those who practice drumming report experiencing an opening of consciousness. Synchronized brain wave activity can activate feelings of euphoria, increased mental command and creativity, what some call a higher state of consciousness.

Physiologically, it has been clinically proven that sustained drumming has benefits common to aerobic exercise by increasing the heart rate & blood flow. Though I wouldn't abandon the gym for a drum, it's nice to know there are beneficial side effects.

According to Tom Bickford, drummer, shaman and drum builder, drumming slows down the brain waves to around 8 cycles per second, which means that drumming heals the human energy field exactly like the laying on of hands. It clears and energizes the Chakras. Drumming puts one in the relaxed, alpha state of meditation, which helps to heal the body.

Well I am a bit skeptical about the Chakra thing, but from experience I can tell you that drumming does clear my mind and really helps me connect. In the case of rhythmic beating with a bottom, it helps me connect with him or her in both a physical and spiritual level.

I like the addition of rhythm to a scene, since it adds another sense to the mix. Most people think SM is all about touch, but it's much more than that. There is the feel of the skin against skin or flogger or other implement, but here is also the smell. The scent of the man or woman you play with or the smell of the leather of the whip or flogger is also part of the experience. Taste often comes into play as well. In a sensual scene, I might put my leather gloved hand across the bottoms mouth. Their tongues explore the taste of the smooth leather gloves. Sometimes I even lick the neck of a sweaty bottom, getting a salty taste of their body and giving them an additional sensual thrill.

Sound always plays a part, even if it's not rhythmic. The slap of skin against skin, the groan of a bottom as they process the pain, or the growls I sometimes find myself omitting without conscious effort when a scene is really getting good. Add to this the new element of rhythm and the whole scene moves in a different direction.

A professor at the University of Ghana's Institute of African Studies says the polyrhythmic drumming of his native Anlo-Ewe people simulates "the dynamics of contrasting moments or emotional stress phenomena likely to occur in actual human existence." In other words the rhythms of the drums can actually prepare people for physical experiences. He notes that intrepidness is bolstered through the drumming and rhythm.

I find that same intrepidness appearing in a scene featuring rhythmic beating. In my experience both bottom and Top not only endure a longer scene, but actually gain energy from the experience. The scene becomes not just a power exchange, but power generating.

How does this work in practice? Well, here's an example.

I had arranged a scene with a friend who I play with often. Bent is a stocky guy, with a good set of muscles and a broad back. He is a big fan of rough body play and likes to get rowdy in the dungeon, in a good way. Brent is known for his often intemperate mouth, and hearing him cursing during a scene means things are going well.

He and I once stopped the play in a dungeon cold when he screamed at me after a particularly painful wallop, "You evil twisted bitch!"

The sound of a bottom cursing at a Top was unheard of in that particular playspace, so people's reactions were abrupt. His voice finally broke the moment of silence that had dropped over the dungeon.

"Evil twisted bitch, Sir," Brent said.

The whole place erupted into laughter. I guess they had never heard a rowdy bottom before?

Brent was the perfect person to try new techniques on, since he is not only ready for just about anything, but vocal enough to let me know what is working and what is not. The scene I had planned would be a little different, but I expected him to give me feedback should things not be going well for him.

I arranged for the music to be changed for the scene, and that alone is no easy thing to do in a public dungeon. Most public dungeons have their own music programs and rarely change them on request. Since I was a partner in this dungeon, that problem was solved.

I selected a piece of trance-dance music that featured a simple tribal style beat. This song lasted about 15 minutes and gradually become more complex in its rhythmic pattern. The beat remained the same tempo, but other rhythms were mixed in, creating the polyrhythmic effect of which the professor spoke. At the end of the song, the beat returned to a simple repeated bass drum beat giving the piece a nice beginning, middle and ending.

I began the scene with Brent facing a St. Andrew's cross. He held on to the eyelets where restraints normally go. I am not a big fan of restraining my bottoms unless they absolutely have to have it. I like for them to be able to move a little and position their hands wherever it is comfortable for them. I have found this prevents a lot of checking for circulation in extremities that are bound, and pauses while restraints are adjusted for the bottoms comfort and safety. I guess I am a lazy Top?

As the music started, I used my hand to stroke Brent's broad back. The initial contact was just to let him get used to my touch and for us to connect physically before the scene really got going. Still, I moved my hands in time to the slow but relentless rhythm of the music, each stroke getting progressively firmer. As my flesh stroked his I felt him moving with the beat, not in a big way, but subtle movements, a slight sway and changing of weight from one foot to another.

The strokes from my hands became more percussive, and gradually I was slapping his back with the full surface of my palm. Again I gradually increased the pressure of each slap still in keeping with the beat of the music. As I slapped I moved around his broad back, varying the spot where I struck, but keeping to the larger muscle ground and avoiding his kidneys, shoulder blades and spinal column.

The tempo began to move into a polyrhythmic beat, with one tempo superimposed in another. I varied my slaps to accommodate the rhythmic change and began adding stronger ones as accent to the milder slaps. The rhythm was infectious and soon both he and I were caught up in the experience. The rest of the dungeon faded away and before long it was just Brent and I and the beats. The beat guided me to begin adding light punches to the pattern. Slap, slap, punch, slap! Moving from his left to his right side, mixing the slaps and punches in tempo to the song.

As the scene built I began punctuating the rhythm with two handed slaps and punches, bringing the full weight of my blows down on him at the same time; both hands slamming against the muscles of his back. Then, I moved back to softer single slaps, building to a big two handed thud again. The scene began rolling like a wave, building and building then crashing with a forceful two handed slap or punch. Each crash was met with a breathless groan from Brent as he absorbed and processed the sensations.

As the song began to wind down, my blows became softer and finally returned to the soft stroking that had begun the scene. The music died out and I stepped forward to feel the warmth of Brent's reddened back. I wrapped my arms around him and pulled him back into my chest, feeling him grind into me still savoring the sensations in his skin and muscles.

As we caught our breath pressed against each other, I heard the sounds of the dungeon return and became aware of our surroundings again. A small crowd stood around us watching and they burst into spontaneous subdued applause as we both looked up and saw them. I smiled and turned Brent to me and kissed him. He responded by dropping to his knees and bending to lick my boots. It's always nice to have a polite boy who appreciates your work.

A Sticky Situation

I guess everyone my age has at least one relative who lived through the Great Depression. I feel lucky that I didn't have to face that dark time in American history because I have seen how its effects colored some of my relative's lives and actions long after that era was gone. I had an Aunt, a second cousin really, who had vivid memories of the Depression and the shortage it brought to her family. The result was that she never wasted anything. It wasn't a bad attitude, and today she would simply be called a recycler, but back in the 1950's she just seemed strange.

When she would attend one of my birthday parties, she fastidiously picked up every scrap of wrapping paper and carefully straightened it out. She folded it neatly and stacked it on a table. She had a whole shelf full of old wrapping paper that she reused for wrapping gifts. It was not unusual to get a gift from her several years in a row with the same paper.

Conversely, I had another relative, this one a real Aunt, who wrapped extravagantly. She delighted in finding new and unusual paper to festoon her gifts. Wrapping to her was as much a part of the gift as the actual gift itself. She taught me the joys of gift wrapping and indirectly some of the surprising uses for wrapping materials.

Cellophane tape fascinated me from an early age. The sticky stuff had a hundred uses, from sealing packages, to repairing tares. When Christmas came, I would help my Aunt wrap packages and I got to be the master of the tape.

She had one of those heavy tape dispensers that made working with cellophane tape easy. Pull, rip and tape! Simple and fast. Of course I rarely did anything simply, and I used to waste as much tape as I used to actually wrap gifts. You could stick the clear stuff to your skin and with a little ingenuity actually use it to modify your appearance. I gave myself tape face-lifts and tape enabled nose jobs. Occasionally I would reassign my own ethnicity and become Asian with tape holding my eyes wide into thin slanted slits.

It was harmless play and the tape never stuck very well to my skin, but I always remembered the experiences I had during gift wrapping season.

That fascination with tape really got a boost as an adult. I also discovered the mysterious and ever useful Duct Tape.

Duct tape is pretty cool stuff. Its smooth grayish silver color makes it seem very industrial and heavy duty. In actuality, it is not all that sticky. In fact I have been told by HVAC professionals that Duct Tape is good for lots of things but is really bad for use on ducts. Apparently the moisture of a heating/cooling system defeats the adhesive in the tape and it literally falls off. That is a nifty fact to remember, but more on that later.

My fascination with duct tape led me to find lots of ways to use it in scenes. The most natural is as a restraint. It's quick and easy to restrain a bottom with duct tape. It's also pretty safe. Duck tape can be cut with no loss of valuable equipment and the bottom can be released almost instantly. It works as a theatrical effect to gag someone, but in reality, duck tape across the mouth is pretty useless. Remember what the HVAC guy said? Moisture makes it loose its adhesion. I once used a strip of duct tape to gag a friend during a scene and within two minutes I watched it fall off his sweat soaked face. So much for all those movies with people being gagged with duct tape!

It was not until I was attending an SM weekend in the wilds of Michigan that I found the best use for duct tape in my play. At this gathering lots of hot men use their inventiveness and talent to create not only a hot play weekend, but a laboratory for new scenes and toys. I have rarely attended this event that I did not learn some new use for an old toy, or even better a new technique to add to my repertoire.

It was one afternoon. The weather was pleasant and I was strolling by a large tent where people did bondage and other scenes that might require tables or platforms. As I rounded the corner of the tent on my way back to my room, I heard a blood curdling scream. Needless to say, my interest was piqued. As I approached a table surrounded by three men, I heard another scream, but this time it was muffled. Seems someone had decided that stuffing the bottoms jock into his mouth would be more pleasant than having permanent ear damage from his screams. As I got closer I expected to see some diabolical device torturing the poor, but willing man on the table. As I got closer I saw almost nothing but a naked man, being held down by two friends as he struggled to process what apparently was intense pain.

Then I saw the reason for his screams. Another man was slowly removing strips of ordinary duct tape from his skin. One by one, he slowly pulled the tape off the bottom and as his screams attested, it was profoundly painful.

I watched for another few minutes from a suitable distance while he finished the scene. Each strip was pulled away from the skin with a deliberate pace so slow that it must have been maddening for the bottom. I was grinning like a kid who had just seen a new toy in the window of a toy store. This was my kind of scene. Very painful. Very controlled, and deceptively simple.

Afterward, the bottom was out of breath, but exceedingly happy. I suspect some of it was the endorphins that must have been coursing through his body, but part of it was from the ability to survive the scene itself. It was a real test of endurance and stamina.

When I returned home, it wasn't long before I had my roll of duct tape out and began plastering it on my legs and arms. Now I am a relatively hirsute bear-type guy. I have never shaved, and enjoy having a certain amount of body hair. I was relieved that very little hair was removed by the tape as I pulled it off. Unfortunately I found there was not as much pain as I expected. Pulling a strip of duct tape from my leg by lifting the end of the strip higher and higher did serve to remove the tape and it was a little painful, but certainly not the kind of pain I witnessed.

I began to experiment with different speeds and found that faster was even less painful. At first I thought that the scene might have been just an anomaly with a bottom who was very sensitive to pain. If memory served, he wasn't even that hairy!

Then I tried pulling the tape across itself, folding the strip back so that only a thin edge of the tape was pulling off the skin at one time. That's when I screamed!

"Motherfucker!"

I caught my breath and tried to continue peeling the tape away in that manner and soon discovered that I couldn't make myself do it. It felt like I was having my skin pulled off rather than the tape. That thin knife edge fold where the tape bent back from the skin served to focus all the adhesive power and the pain potential in one spot and it was amazing!

I waited a while before continuing and then discovered that my sweating had diminished the effect of the adhesive so much that it was merely annoying rather than painful. I looked at my watch and found that it had been about 20 minutes since I started. For me that was apparently the magic number for when my skin developed enough moisture to release the tape.

What that experimentation did was give me an idea of not only the pain levels that were possible, but a good time frame for how long to keep the tape on. Unlike clothespins or some other pain scenes, this one was all about removing the tape. It was controlled by how the strips were pulled off and had a built in safety feature. If the bottom absolutely could not stand any more, just wait long enough and the tape will come off with less pain.

I had also a few fears of this scene becoming a depilatory technique, but upon examining my arm I found very few hairs missing. The ones in the adhesive of the used tape were probably those hairs that would have fallen out by themselves very soon. I do believe that hair plays a big part in the level of pain. Though since I first started doing these tape scenes, I have played with women and shaved men, they report some pain, but none as intense as those with lots of hair.

Now my biggest problem was finding someone who absolutely loved an intense scene. I would also need a few friends to help hold the person down, because the instinct to struggle, that fight or flight thing, would be very strong. I feared bondage like ropes or restraints might lead to injury since they didn't give enough.

At a play party the following month I found a friend who had a distinct affinity for pain scenes as well as being more than a bit of an exhibitionist. Sean was medium build and had a nice covering of fine red hair. I spent some time talking about what I wanted to try with him over a couple of soft drinks and munchies in the social area of the dungeon.

He seemed skeptical that something as innocent as duct tape could be the source of the most excruciating pain scenes I had even witnessed. I reassured him that it was not as innocent as he thought, and reminded him that if at any time during the scene he needed to stop to not hesitate to let me know.

That was all it took to get him to agree. He had no problem with the safe-word aspect of the scene, but the way I had brought it up made the whole thing a personal challenge to him. He wanted to prove to me and everyone else that either this wasn't so bad, or he was able to endure the worst thing imaginable. It was almost as though I had tried to manipulate him into doing the scene. Who me?

We entered the dungeon and secured a padded massage table for the scene. I had two other men join me to help out as human restraints, though Sean kept saying he wouldn't need them. As he took off his clothes and hopped up on the table, I looked at the nice patterns of red hair that highlighted the shape of his muscles. This was going to be fun!

I took a few moments to let Sean settle in and then placed my hand on his chest. I felt his breathing and waited a moment to let it slow to a nice reasonable pace. I asked him if he had any allergies to duct tape or adhesive, and he shook his head. During this time I again reassured him that he should let me know at any time if he wanted me to stop. He smiled and slyly said, "We won't be stopping until you are worn out."

I took this as my cue to start. I began by holding the roll of duct tape near his face. Then for dramatic effect I pulled off a strip about 18 inches long. The sound of the tape unrolling has become one of my favorites! Since that evening the low ripping roar of duct tape is an erotic melody that raises goose bumps and other things on my body.

I put the first strip along the outside of his right arm, sealing the tape firmly against his skin. As I did this, I watched the expression on his face change from cocky self-assuredness to the beginnings of what later was to be a deep and genuine fear.

The next strip went on the opposite arm. Working slowly and unrolling each strip directly in front of his face to give him the maximum aural and visual effect, I put strips up the tops and sides of his thighs. Then I added two strips along the top and sides of each calf. I was consciously working to place tape in areas of the body where there are an abundance of nerve endings. By doing this I was assured of having the greatest effect when I removed them.

I finished him off with 5 strips down his chest just to the top of his pubic hair. I refrained from putting any tape on his genitals or pubic region. It was too sensitive and would probably become too moist for much effect.

Once the last strip was in place, I leaned in close to him and whispered, "Hang on tight, it's going to be a bumpy ride!"

Sean laughed nervously and then looked into my eyes. I saw the confidence disappear, and all that was left was fear and some confusion. Without breaking our gaze, I picked the edge of the tape strip on his right arm and held it firmly in my fingers. Then slowly I pulled it back over itself, peeling the tape away from Sean's skin with a deliberate slowness. Almost immediately I saw his eyes blaze with the fire of pain. He wailed as the tape pulled away from his skin, occasionally pulling at the roots of the hair on his arm. The two friends who had agreed to help sprang into action and held his extremities firm as he began to kick and squirm. It took all their strength to keep him stable, and at times I wondered if the massage table could stand the strain.

Once the first strip was free, I allowed him to catch his breath. He was panting fast as I looked back into his eyes and saw some of the old defiance begin to appear.

"Intense?"

He smiled, still shaking with adrenaline, "oh, guess you could call it that, you evil twisted fuck."

I returned his smile, "I'll take that as a compliment."

My fingers had already grasped the top of another strip, this one in the center of his chest. As I started to pull it away, his face burned red and his eyes starred into mine with a fearsome anger.

"Oh fuck!" He struggled to form more words but all that came out were yells and unintelligible shrieks.

As the scene proceeded and each strip was removed, he continued to struggle and writhe. Having helpers was about the only way I could have done this scene; restraints would have either broken or harmed

Sean as he struggled. I looked at the two men helping out and saw that both of them were experiencing the same power rush that I was. Sean was emitting energy like a battery. His screams and struggles had aroused all of us. I noticed that my helpers had uncomfortable lumps in their jeans similar to mine. This was damn hot!

I gave Sean another break before moving to the last two strips. These were on his chest, and I intended to pull them off in tandem. I could see the fear beginning to grow in him as I told him what I planned. As a concession to his fear, I told him he could let me know how intense the scene was by physical means. I took his hand and placed it directly between my legs. He grabbed by balls through the fabric of the jeans and squeezed. This would be my barometer. The harder he squeezed, the more pain he was feeling. It also gave me a chance to get in on the scene in a physical way.

I leaned close to his ear and whispered a few final words before starting to pull the tape off his chest.

"This is going to hurt you more than it does me."

He squeezed my balls and replied, "but it's gonna hurt you a little as well, I promise."

I laughed and began pulling the tape strips from his chest with both hands. As they slowly peeled away, Sean shrieked like a wounded animal. His grip on my balls had been forgotten in the flood of sensations that washed over him. It wasn't until the last few inches of tape that he realized he was still in control of at least two things. My nuts!

I am not sure who growled the loudest; because my ears were filled with my own roar as I pulled the last of the duct tape from Sean's chest. My balls were aching from his grip but I finished the scene.

As soon as the last of the tape pulled away, Sean's hand fell away from my aching nuts. He was spent and panting. Both of us were beginning to sweat, and my two helpers looked exhausted as well. I leaned over Sean and embraced him, getting one last surge of energy from him after the scene. He kissed my neck and then began chuckling. Soon all of us were laughing uncontrollably. The body's opiate factory had cranked into overdrive and we were all high from the endorphins.

As I helped Sean to his feet, and escorted him to a chair he whispered in my ear.

"I will never be able to go into a hardware store without getting a hard on again."

The Kindest Cut of All

My father was a scientist. He was a researcher in the field of Microbiology, and he tried to encourage my interest in medicine from an early age. One of the ways was to give me gifts that had scientific value. Today these learning toys are common place, but back in the dark ages of the 1950's kids toys were intended to amuse not educate. Because of this I also received some more adult gifts. I got a microscope around the age of 8 and it was not the plastic kind kids get today; it was a full blown medical student version. I spent a lot of time looking at the world through this wonderful toy.

More interestingly, my father brought home specimens from the lab for me to see. I had everything from Streptococcus to Pseudomonas both very nasty diseases, the first causing pneumonia and the second an opportunistic disease that accounts for just over 10% of all hospital-acquired infections. Today, my bedroom and my collection of specimens would probably be considered a biohazard. Still it was very cool to be able to really impress the class when it came to show and tell.

Because of this background I have always been very conscious of the possibilities of transmitting disease in the dungeon. For a long time that concern steered me away from any activity involving blood or invasive activity. I finally got over that block surprisingly because of my own work as a director of medical documentaries and industrial programs.

I had a chance to shoot many instructional videos for a major medical supply manufacturer. Ironically, one of the products, a high-level disinfectant chemical was originally developed with research done by my father!

While shooting these videos, a great number of which involved filming actual surgery, I became fascinated with surgical technique. I was working closely with one of the country's leading authorities on sterile technique and operating room protocol. She was an OR nurse with lots of credentials. I learned how to work in a sterile environment and how to do everything from correctly wash your hands to infection control during invasive procedures.

One of the most fascinating things I found during this was how few surgeons use really good sterile technique. We had to sometimes ask surgeons to perform the simple act of donning a pair of gloves several times before they did it correctly. The other thing I found was that even though some surgeons had pretty lousy sterile technique, their patients seemed to survive without complications.

Though I would never have the patience to be an Operating Room nurse, I have learned how to minimize the risks of contamination and infection in invasive procedures. I have put this knowledge to good use in the dungeon. So far I have had no reports of infections or complications resulting from any blood or invasive play in which I have been involved.

My other really cool educational toy I received as a child was a kit of medical tools. Though I thought they were surgical tools, they were in actuality a dissection kit. Still they were shiny and inside a nifty little leather case. With these I was a mad scientist!

One tool in this kit that got my utmost respect yet held the most fascination was the scalpel. This was the kind used in actual surgery, with a disposable blade and a heavy stainless steel handle. I was lucky to have never cut myself with this sharp and very unsterile tool. I ended up using it for everything from dissections of insects to cutting balsa wood for model airplanes. Needless to say, it didn't remain very sharp for long.

Still I believe that scalpel started my lifelong fascination with knives and shiny sharp things. The other possibility is that I was a bird in a former existence.

Today, I still love shiny things and sharp things. Both work well in the dungeon, of you take care and use proper technique. Again I feel I need to add a word of warning.

> *Any activity that involves breaking he skin whether by piercing or cutting carries with it an inherent risk. I am talking about infections. The skin is on our bodies for a reason. It protects us from foreign organisms. Bacteria and viruses can be most easily transmitted through the bloodstream, cutting and piercing directly affect that function in our bodies. Anything that is on the skin or the instrument used for the invasive play can potentially enter your body. That means that extra care must be used when doing this kind of play.*

> *I do not advocate anyone doing this kind of play without proper training by a qualified instructor. There are a whole host of infections that can get into your bloodstream during this kind of scene, from HIV/AIDS to the much talked about flesh-eating bacteria, Group A streptococcus. Scary? You bet and I tell you this in order to emphasize how important proper technique and instruction is. Use common sense and find someone who can teach you if you really want to try some of these activities. You have been warned and anything you do is at your own risk.*

Now, that said, I want to tell you a story. This particular scene took place at an event I attended and it left a deep impression on me. It is a really interesting and theatrical way of doing what is commonly called a cutting. Needless to say, it involves sharp shiny things!

I was one of the few men attending the workshop, and from the looks of the rest of the crowd, most were leatherdykes. I use that term as an endearment, because I have learned many of my best techniques from my leatherdyke sisters.

The woman giving the workshop started with the customary explanation of the safety precautions needed and the risks involved. She emphasized the need to know the health condition of the person you are playing with for a variety of reasons. First among them was to know if they had any bleeding problems, like hemophilia or if they had taken any kind of blood thinners. Blood thinners make clotting much slower and in a cutting scene that means everything. Something as simple as an aspirin can inhibit the body's ability to clot quickly, thus it is often prescribed for people middle aged and older as a proactive way to fend off strokes. Additionally it's always good to know if the person you are playing with has any diseases or conditions that would require special consideration.

Since all blood play or piercing should be treated as though the bottom has a communicable disease, precautions against cross contamination should be the same no matter what their health. (In the medical world this is called *universal precautions*) However if they have a compromised immune system they may be more vulnerable to opportunistic infections and that risk should be discussed.

Once the health questions were out of the way, the scene began. The bottom, actually a longtime friend of the woman doing the workshop, removed her shirt and laid on a padded table that had been on hand for the demonstration. The Top then donned a pair of latex-free exam gloves and used a surgical preparation to clean the skin. At the time this was an iodine based product, but today there are better products available for this purpose. I suggest checking with a local piercer or tattoo artist to find the most up to date product for cleaning the skin prior to play.

She started in a circular motion working from the center of the back outward. Several sterile gauze sponges were used and within a few minutes the back of the bottom was ready for the scene. Another nice thing about cleaning the skin, other than the medical reasons is the intimacy it conveys. It gives the Top and bottom a chance to connect in a physical way prior to the start of the scene. I like making this connection since it opens the way for the power exchange that follows during the scene.

Once the cleaning was done, the Top donned a fresh pair of gloves and opened a disposable scalpel. This kind was made with a plastic handle and a steel blade. The entire scalpel was meant to be discarded after use.

She moved close to the back of her bottom and lightly sketched out a few lines. She did this deliberately and with precision, cutting only a very shallow incision into the skin. The bottom winced and moved a little at the first cuts, but soon settled and was calm. I knew she was already starting to feel the bodies built in pain controls kicking into high gear. Endorphins and other natural opioids were doing their job to relieve the pain of the incisions. Even though incisions are not as painful as some other play, they affect the body differently. The body senses that the skin has been compromised and responds fast.

She continued making very shallow cuts in a growing pattern on the bottoms back, checking in with her occasionally to make sure she was alright. So far there was almost no blood. The skin of the back is pretty thick and since the cuts only went through the first thin layers of skin, a layer with very few capillaries that carry blood, bleeding was slow to start.

After a few more cuts the Top had finished her pattern. Then she did something that really made the bottoms back start responding to the cuts. She pressed on the skin and gently stretched it a little with both hands. This gentle pulling started the blood flowing.

I am not talking about a gush of the red stuff, just a slow seeping to the surface of blood in the lines of the cuts.

Now she began a completely different part of the scene, one intended to affect the audience watching rather than the bottom she was playing with. Needless to say, this part got my full attention. Sometimes I am such a voyeur!

She took a fresh roll of paper towels and began laying them on the back of the bottom. Once the paper had absorbed a little of the blood, she picked it up and showed it to the group. It was a beautiful symmetrical pattern of a double headed ax surrounded by a ring of flame shaped lines.

Then she pulled a string that had been suspended above her and took a pair of tiny clothespins and hung the "print" from the line. She then proceeded to take another impression from the bottoms back. Each successive one was slightly different as the blood flow subsided. Each one she hung along the string, which was strung like a clothesline down the center aisle of the room. The line had pulleys at both ends allowing her to move the "prints" down the aisle as she worked.

A total of over a dozen paper towels festooned the room before she was done.

At the end of her printmaking she used a sterile gauze pad to wipe the bottoms back, and then she applied a topical antibiotic and sealed her back with a transparent dressing. As she finished she reminded everyone not to touch the "prints" since they represented a potential biohazard.

After the demonstration, she gathered the prints and put them inside a plastic bag for safekeeping. I suspect there are many of my readers who will be horrified at this scene. I remind you that it is not intended as instructive, but merely a story of a very dramatic scene I witnessed. As far as I am concerned there were acceptable risks involved. I understand that strictly speaking the audience may have been exposed to possible contact with body fluids, but no one actually was. I suspect there is more risk attending a prize fight and sitting ringside. I have heard tales from people who have been splattered with sweat and blood from the fighters, and they received no safety warnings.

I had a unique opportunity to witness both a delightful pain scene and an impromptu performance art piece. Anyone who knows me very well will understand that this is a double win in my book. Anytime you can have a scene that is not only fun for the participants, but enlightens and entertains those watching, you have done something positive.

Playing Between the Ears

Sometimes pain is more imagined than real. The imagination is really one of the most powerful sex toys we have and some people never use it. I am a firm believer in the adage, "that which is used develops and that which is unused fades away". In my circle of friends these kinds of scene are called "Mind Fucks". They consist of BDSM practical jokes for lack of a better explanation, but they can still be very erotic and effective, even though there is an element of deception.

We play with this kind of thing every time we enter a dungeon. We are not in a real medieval dungeon where people are tortured and killed; we are in a room or space designated as a consensual play space for our activities. When we tie someone up in our bedroom, they are not real captives. It is consensual bondage and their release is always at hand should there be an emergency or they simply want to end the scene.

Our play requires what magicians call a "suspension of disbelief". In other words, we accept a situation that is clearly artificial as reality for a period of time. It's that ability to live in the fantasy that makes our scenes sexy and exciting. The first time I viewed a BDSM scene at a public play party, I was supremely underwhelmed. The participants were average looking and the activities they were engaging in seemed tame and uninspiring. It was only later when I spoke to them and understood what was going on in their heads that I found it exciting.

So, I ask you to suspend your disbelief for a while as you read the next story. I will tell it from the standpoint of a Top, since a friend and I were cooperating in the scene with a bottom who wanted something special and different.

We were outdoors, at a campground filled with hundreds of hot kinky men. It was the kind of gathering I gravitate towards. I really like playing outside and in an atmosphere of raw testosterone that an all male event brings.

Roy had told my friend Rick and I that he wanted an extreme bondage scene. Something that involved suspension as well. Conveniently, Rick owned a leather bondage suit that was just the right size for Roy and there were numerous places to rig up a block and tackle in the campgrounds.

I started early and set up the hoist. It was a rope device that consisted of a block and tackle with a special locking device on it to prevent slipping. By the time I had it set up, and attached to a sturdy tree limb, Roy and Rick arrived with the bondage suit.

It was a mild day, with a good breeze that would make the leather suit tolerable. Sweating is something that is unavoidable in a bondage suit, but doing it in a hot environment is a recipe for disaster.

Rick had Roy undress and step into the suit. Then he started slowly and methodically buckling him in. The suit fit over Roy's body like a glove, covering every inch with leather. As I helped Rick buckle the suit up, Roy's skin began disappearing, replaced by the shiny leather of the suit.

This particular suit had been custom made for Rick, and had various attachment points and reinforcements to allow the person wearing it to be suspended from a variety of points. As I zipped the front closed and pulled the straps across Roy's chest taught I asked him to take a deep breath. This assured he would be able to breathe once the straps were in place. Otherwise he would be bound with empty lungs and only shallow breaths would be possible.

Rick finished buckling and zipping the arms closed and then he attached them to hooks on the sides of the suit. Finally after reaching Ricks neck, we both pulled a leather hood over his head. This hood had a removable blindfold and a zipper across the mouth to allow Roy to take fluids occasionally as the scene progressed. There was also a nose hole and sufficient ventilation to allow unrestricted breathing throughout the scene.

The last step was to lay Roy down so we could suspend him. Rick had brought his sleeping bag as a pad for Roy and we both maneuvered him onto it directly below the hoist I had set up earlier. We let him lay on the pad face up for a while as we continued preparations.

For a person who is a bondage enthusiast, just being in the firm constraints of the suit was a scene in itself. You were at once restricted in your movements and sensations, yet free to experience the feel and smell of the leather and the heightened senses brought about by the temporary loss of your sight. Some friends who enjoy this kind of bondage tell me it's like floating, somewhat similar to a "float tank" experience.

While Roy floated, Rick and I prepared the suspension. We attached a metal bar designed to hold a person's weight to the main line of the hoist. From that bar we would attach a web of rope to the attachment points of the suit. To do this we had to turn Roy face down. We carefully maneuvered him onto his stomach and began weaving lengths of rope through the attachment rings of the suit. There were about ten rings on each side of the suit. These were fastened to reinforcement straps that passed around Roy's body at strategic points. They were designed to distribute his weight over a broad area and prevent any constrictions.

As we tied the last of the ropes to the metal suspension bar, Rick and I paused to catch our breath. Elaborate bondage can be hard work for the Top, or in this case Tops. It had taken us almost a half an hour to get Roy into the suit and get him ready to be hoisted off the ground. We slowly pulled the rope on the hoist and Roy's body began to move upward. Slowly, inch by inch we moved him off the ground, checking to be sure the tension on the rope web was evenly distributed. For Roy, the experience was one of being levitated, or so he told us later.

He felt he was floating in a leather cocoon. He had no idea of how high above the ground he was hanging or exactly what was going on around him.

In actuality, Roy was only about three feet off the ground. The actual height was not important; his experience would be the same since his senses were dulled by the bondage suit.

Rick and I sat down in a couple of lawn chairs and enjoyed a couple of cigars, downwind of Roy. The time we spent would allow Roy to float in his own little world, and for him that was the best part of the bondage experience. We kept Roy in our sights and stayed alert for any signs of struggle that might signal a problem. All we saw was his steady breathing and an occasional muscle twitch in his legs or arms.

One of the joys of playing outdoors is the surroundings. The sights and sounds of nature make the experience more robust. In the case of a sensory deprivation scene the loss of that natural world makes it more intense as well. The big problem with the great outdoors is the presence of lots of voyeurs. In this case, the human voyeurs were no problem. Having a scene in a semi-public setting you have to expect people will watch. It's part of the fun of these kinds of events. Though everyone there was a consensual participant in the weekend activities, it has an element of public exhibitionism that makes a scene a little more exciting.

The other voyeurs are less friendly. The whole weekend we had been invaded by what are commonly called "Sweat Bees". These annoying little insects were not particularly dangerous, and would only sting if smashed against your skin. Though there were none around at the moment I was on the lookout for them. I have a particular dislike for stinging insects.

That's when an idea struck me. Since the scene so far had absolutely no element of pain involved, I wondered if I might be able to introduce one without totally breaking the scene for Roy. I whispered my idea to Rick who was barely able to contain his conspiratorial laughter.

The bondage suit had several zippers that held coverings in place over specific areas of the body. One, not surprisingly, was directly over the crotch of the suit. Rick and I moved closer to Roy and gently dragged our fingertips over the leather suit. Our fingers caused tremors to ripple through Rick's body. The introductions of sensations, no matter how slight after being deprived for a time makes them seem all the more profound.

After toying with him for a time, we unzipped the panel over his crotch. His cock sprang out in a full erection. Apparently the sensations were erotic to Roy and that was a good thing!

We toyed with his erect cock and teased his balls for a few moments, then allowed him to float once again. I knew he could hear us through the leather hood, so I started a very quiet conversation with Rick. It was part of my plan, and we kept our voices just loud enough that Roy could hear some of what we said.

I commented on the Sweat Bees and how persistent they were. Rick shared a story about a boy who had been stung by one of the bees while he was bound to a cross. It was not a true story, but I did notice Roy stiffen a bit at the mention of it. I then conjectured that it would be interesting if we could get one of the bees to land on Roy's cock.

Roy really stiffened at this suggestion, but so did his penis. Something about that idea scared Roy and excited him at the same time. I reached into my toy bag and pulled out a tube of lube. I then asked Rick if he would go get that honey he kept in his tent for sweetening his morning tea. At the same time I pointed to the tube of lube. Rick got the idea and noisily ran off, pretending to go over to his tent. In actuality he just retreated a few feet and then returned.

I elaborated the story by telling Rick, in reality for Roy's benefit, that I was going to smear some honey on Roy's dick and see if we could attract a few bees. At that, Roy really responded. He wasn't really struggling, but his twitching became pronounced.

I carefully stroked some of the clear lube on his cock as Rick plucked a few blades of grass. He held the grass in a small bundle and as we discussed the impending arrival of the bees, he drew closer to Roy's slippery cock.

"Oh my God!" Rick gasped. "It's working, look."

I struggled to keep from laughing as he took the grass and gently touched it to Roy's cock.

The tiny grass blades must have felt like a bee landing on his penis, because Roy bucked as soon as Rick touched him.

"Hope it doesn't sting him," I added as I pulled a Wartenberg wheel from my toy bag. (These are the pin wheels that neurologists use to test reflexes and nerve sensitivity. They are a staple of my sensation play.)

I moved closer and then touched one of the sharp points to Roy's cock right next to the spot where Rick was holding the grass.

Roy's scream was loud even through the leather hood. Though there was no real damage Roy believed he had been stung by a bee and on the most sensitive part of his body. He was panting and yelping like a hurt puppy.

I quickly took a towel and wrapped his still erect cock, then stuffed it back into the bondage suit and zipped the panel shut. His writhing had calmed down some and both Rick and I assured him we had chased the bees away, all the time trying not to laugh.

We lowered Roy slowly toward the sleeping bag and finally got him back on the ground. After carefully removing the ropes that held him we rolled him over and unfastened his arms and legs. Still in the suit but able to sit up we helped him into a sitting position before removing his hood.

"Close your eyes," I told him, "it's going to be bright."

We unlaced the leather hood and removed it from his sweat soaked head. As he slowly opened his eyes, his face was beaming. Rick hugged him and held him while I began opening the buckles of the suit.

"Oh my God," Roy said, "that was incredible, thank you."

He continued to hug Rick and then me as we continued to extricate him from the suit.

Roy was shaking with the adrenaline that coursed through his body from the imagined pain of the "bee sting". He was still shaking a little when we finally got him completely out of the suit.

As he eagerly examined his cock and found no damage he breathed a sigh of relief and began laughing. He continued to thank Rick and me for our efforts to create a unique fantasy experience for him and later he thanked Rick in a more intimate way.

The whole experience had been a really effective mind fuck for him as well as a good bondage experience. The addition of the "bee sting" trick though not actually painful in any physical sense, had triggered all the body's pain and survival mechanisms and might as well have been real. That is the most profound example of suspension of disbelief I have ever seen.

The combination of sensory deprivation and the fantasy we created for Roy managed to fool not only his conscious mind, but his subconscious minds as well. Who says make believe is just for kids?

Love and Pinches

My first experiences with the effects of pain were as a child. The story of playing with clothespins and my profound experience with them has lead to a lifelong fascination with the pain and pleasure continuum.

In my journey, one of my favorite activities has continued to be the use of clamps and clothespins. What started as clips on the nipples progressed to using hundreds of clothespins to engulf and enrapture my partners. I like to approach a clothespin scene as a chance to bring my partner and myself to a "peak" experience. What I share here is my understanding of how that process works and a few of the techniques and toys I use to achieve that goal. My methods are not for everybody. The intense experiences I have come to love using clothespins border on "edge play", and should be approached with caution. The beauty of clips and clamps is that they are not all or nothing toys. They can be used for milder stimulation or as an adjunct to a larger scene.

Pinching, the act of compressing the upper layer of the skin produces an immediate sensation. Depending on the pressure, area of skin compressed, and number of nerve endings at a particular location, the sensation can be only mildly stimulating or extremely intense. The ability to control and vary this sensation in a precise way makes SM play with clips, clamps and clothespins so popular.

I am not a doctor, though I do sometimes play one in the dungeon, so I am not going to try to give a precise medical and anatomical explanation of the physiology of compression. What I can do is give a short description of the general principals involved. To do that I'll illustrate with a story.

The lovely Danielle is standing in line at Le Cinema. Behind her is Maurice, the saucy and annoying French Politician. Danielle, wearing the fashion of the day, a micro skirt, reaches down to pick up her purse that she dropped.

Monsieur Politician, unable to control his urges sees Danielle's derrière and gives her a flirtatious pinch.

When skin is compressed or pinched, the nerve endings in the upper layers of the skin send information through the central nervous system alerting the brain that something is going on.

"Mon Dieu!" cries Danielle.

Depending on the intensity of the sensation, that signal triggers an appropriate response in the brain and the body takes action.

Turing she catches Monsieur Le Politician with a glancing blow from her purse to his head.

At that point his nervous system takes over, but that, and the ensuing trial are another story. Meanwhile, the nerves, having received no further stimulation gradually stop firing off their messages, and the pain in Danielle's *derrière* subsides.

Intense stimulation or mild trauma to the upper layers of the skin causes the body's nerves to buzz, somewhat like an alarm bell. They send off signal after signal to the brain, until the stimulation subsides. For a brief period after the stimulation has subsided they remain in a heightened state of readiness.

"Merde!", exclaims Danielle, as she sits down in her seat in the theater.

The nerves are remembering Monsieur Le Politician's crude advances, and let the brain know in no uncertain terms.

Now, leaving Danielle to enjoy the movie, let's look at how that same process works when the compression is done by a clamp or clothespin.

For this example we will look in on Rick and Bryan during a scene in their upstairs playroom. Though the men are involved in an elaborate scene, we'll concentrate specifically on Bryan's left nipple.

Rick has been applying various forms of stimulation to this small area of skin with the desired results. Bryan's nipple is erect and filled with blood, making it an ideal subject for this demonstration. The heightened stimulation has alerted the brain that something is going on. In response, the brain triggers the circulatory system to supply extra blood to the tissue in the nipple. This tissue, much like the tissue of a woman's nipple, and a man's penis, is spongy. When blood flows into the tissue, it causes the area to become rigid, thus the name "erectile tissue". (Why the body does this probably has something to do with child-rearing, but that's too grizzly for me to think about.)

> *Rick cannot resist doing something to this nice perky nipple, so he reaches into his toy bag and produces a forceps.*
>
> *"You wouldn't?" exclaims Bryan.*
>
> *Rick does. He grips the nipple in the rubber padded clamps and starts to squeeze the forceps closed.*
>
> *"You bastard!" moans Bryan.*

Bryan's reaction is caused by the same series of events that happened in Danielle's body, but because he is in a receptive mood, the sensation, though painful, is invigorating rather than annoying.

The tight grip of the forceps continues to squeeze Rick's nipple and keeps the nerves busy sending message after message to the brain.

> *"Relax", chuckles Rick, "it won't hurt for long."*

Knowing his craft, Rick is right. After a certain amount of time, the nerve begins to slow down its alarm. Blood has been forced away from the nerve by the pressure of the clamps, and the brain has begun triggering another response. It is furiously creating opioids, endorphins and enkephlins to slow down the alarm signals. These natural pain killers don't affect the area being clamped, but rather dampen the alarm bells going off in the brain.

"How are you doing?" whispers Rick.

"Much better, Sir", mumbles Bryan, now concentration on another part of his anatomy.

The nerves in Bryan's nipple have become numb. From lack of blood and compression, they have ceased sending messages. Cutting of the blood supply to the nerves for extended periods of time can cause permanent damage, but Rick knows that he can leave the clamp on for up to 20 minutes without any problems.

Every scene involving compression is really a two part experience. The first part is the application of the clamps or clips. With that comes the initial stimulation and pain, but as in Bryan's nipple, that part ends when the nerves go numb. The second part of the scene is equally invigorating. As the clamps are removed the whole stimulation process begins again, but much faster than before.

"I think your poor little nipple is ready for that mean old clamp to come off," mocks Rick with a sadistic chuckle.

"Whatever you think is best, Sir", Bryan says with a tremble in his voice.

As Rick's hands grasp the forceps, he gently caresses Bryan's chest. This is the calm before the storm.

When Rick opens the jaws of the clamp, the tightly compressed tissue of Bryan's nipple retains the shape of the surface of the clamp, much like the folds of a sheet often imprint themselves on your face while sleeping. This is because both blood and water in the tissue has been forced out, deflating the area of the skin that was compressed.

As the body's fluids rush back in to fill the void, the nerves snap back to attention and start doing their job again.

"Mother fucker!" cries Bryan.

Bryan is paraphrasing the message sent to his brain by the nerves in his nipple. Once again the brain's chemical factory cranks up and goes into overdrive producing pain killers. Even though there is no longer any trauma in the area of Bryan's nipple, the nerves remember and keep sending alarms.

Rick loves to watch Bryan's face twist into agony because he knows the fireworks going off in Bryan's body right now. He slowly reaches out his fingers and moves toward Bryan's throbbing nipple.

As with Danielle's pinched derriere, Bryan's nipple is on red alert, remembering the pain. This is part of the body's protective system to avoid further pain. Even small stimulation can feel almost as intense as the moment the clamp was removed.

"Damn you, you sadistic mother fucker...Sir" Bryan is screaming now, but he is also laughing as Rick presses his nipple hard into his palm.

The overload of endorphins and other natural opioids can sometimes lead to euphoria. This effect lasts for several minutes, and because it can be very strong depending on the amount of stimulation, it is best to allow for a "cool-down" period after any scene of this kind. Players should not be allowed to drive or operate machinery too soon after a clamp or clothespin scene.

Bryan falls into Rick's arms and they lay together on the bed. Rick can feel Bryan trembling with delight and he basks in the amazing energy from his lover's body.

So with the help of these two examples, we've seen the basic principles of any scene involving clips, clamps or clothespins. And so what is one of the simplest of toys can become a very effective tool for creating intense sensations in precise locations. Now here is how it can be taken it to the next level.

Gerry had been corresponding with one of my friends for a while. He had an idea of a scene that would be both a challenge for him and a real peak experience. Knowing my proclivity for clothespins, my friend thought I was the logical choice for a Top for this fantasy, and for that I will be eternally grateful.

Gerry wanted to do a scene using 200 clothespins, all applied to his body above the waist. So far it was interesting but not particularly spectacular, since I had done a scene like that to myself as a demonstration of SM technique in a local leather bar. Gerry's twist on the scene was unique. He wanted all the pins to come off at the same time. For similar scenes I often used "zippers" or clothespins strung on a cord that came of sequentially when the cord was pulled, thus making a zipping sound. These were intense play and very painful as the wooden clips pulled off the skin.

A zipper of 200 clothespins would be almost impossible to achieve, since the length of the cord would be far longer than could be pulled off in one tug. Gerry had the solution.

He had prepared loops of cord with ten clothespins on each. These we called "rippers" since they allowed the pins to be ripped off more or less simultaneously. With careful planning, 20 of these rippers cold be positioned so that the loops could be slipped through the fingers of the Top's hand and removed in one big pull.

Gerry and I pulled together the materials needed and managed to fulfill his fantasy scene at another annual event for gay leathermen. More SM in the great outdoors!

The afternoon of the scene, the sun was shining brightly. In a small glade the run committee had set up scaffolding for use by the attendees. Gerry and I selected a good spot near the scaffold and began laying out our tools. We laid down a couple of towels and began arranging the rippers on neat rows where they would be easily accessible.

Each row of pins was carefully arranged to avoid tangling. The loops varied in length according to where they would go on Gerry's body. Rows of pins that were to be put on his chest had shorter loops than those for his arms. This would allow me to hold all the cords taught for the final rip.

Gerry took off his shirt and leaned back against the scaffold. He wanted to do the scene with no bondage or restrictions. I began putting the pins on his outstretched arms. I have found working with the extremities first makes a clothespin scene go smoother. The arms are far less threatening a spot for this play than the nipples or chest, and it also allows the body to start its natural opiod production going before the more painful areas are affected.

I put two strings of ten clothespins each down the length of his left forearm and then repeated the process with the right forearm. I worked quickly, but at a pace slow enough to allow him to adjust to the sensations. Once these areas were covered, I started on the upper arms. Here there was room for three rows on each arm. Gerry's skin was perfect for this kind of play since he had a low body fat percentage and very supple skin.

Now I started on his chest. I positioned a row of pins down the curve of his pectorals, fitting the pins as close as I could. I repeated this on the opposite side of his chest with another row of ten pins. Next I added 2 additional rows across his upper chest. These stretched the skin and left little room for any more on that part of his body. Luckily, he had plenty of room from the chest down to his waist, and here I managed to fit the last 6 rows of clothespins, three on each side of his stomach.

By the time I had finished putting on the last pin, Gerry was already flying. He smiled at me as I carefully began looping the cords through my fingers. I had ten cords on each had, two on each finger.

Once I was ready, I looked Gerry directly in the eye. He steadied himself with his hands, grasping the steel rods of the scaffolding. As I drew the tension tighter on the cords, Gerry nodded. I could see the fiery pain in his eyes and a little fear as he imagined the experience that was to come. I nodded to assure him that he could do this and I would be with him every second of the scene.

Before I pulled the pins, Gerry said one final thing.

"I want to do this without making a sound," he whispered.

"You will." I assured him.

"I am going to pull on the count of three," I said as I felt everything around us fade into darkness. There was just me and Gerry and the cords in my hands.

"One"

His eyes stared into mine with an incredible intensity.

"Two"

He let out a final breath.

"Three"

I pulled both hands back as fast as I could; moving downward to make sure the clothespins didn't hit him me as they popped off his body.

Everything moved in slow motion. I saw the clothespins slip from his skin and tumble through the air, falling to my sides still dangling from the cords. I saw his face contort into what seemed to be a scream, but there was no sound except his sudden intake of breath. I saw his skin creased with 200 little symmetrical square marks where the jaws of the clothespins had compressed the skin.

I dropped the cords and moved closer to him. My fear was that he might pass out from the sudden trauma. He opened his eyes again and met my stare. As I moved closer I refrained from touching him, knowing how much pain he already was experiencing form the blood rushing back into the skin where it had been pinched.

He began breathing with a shakiness that came from the incredible sensations he had experienced. I moved closer and extended my hands, the fingers wiggling as though I was about to touch his skin. I was teasing him with the possibility of more sensation when he finally burst into laughter.

I hugged him to me, feeling the energy he was giving off, pressing his chest into mine and making the pinched spots surge with renewed pain. He hugged me back as the world came back into focus around us. That's when I heard the sound of applause. Apparently we had drawn a crowd of curious onlookers all of whom had vicariously experienced the scene we just completed.

Later over a cold glass of water, Gerry told me how delighted he was with the whole scene. I too was very glad to have been a part of his fantasy and thanked him for the opportunity.

The only downside of that scene was the effect it had on my play for the rest of the event. Apparently, the people who watched us thought the whole thing had been my idea, and they became too intimidated to engage in any play with me.

I gained a reputation as a "monster" player at that event, and my ego just never let me tell people that the whole thing had been Gerry's idea, until now.

Tales of a Cat

So far, I have not really delved into what most folks think of as traditional SM practices. Whips and floggers, paddles and canes are certainly in my toy bag. I enjoy the more traditional style scenes as much as the next sadist, but so much has been written on these topics already, I don't think I have much to add as far as techniques are concerned.

Though I do know how to handle a single-tail whip, I am far from an expert and so I leave those scenes to people more skilled. Canes and paddles have their place, and I can wield them with equal aplomb. I even learned the English Headmaster's technique of delivering "ten of his best." But to be honest, canes never really did much for me as a top. I suspect it is the stinging quality of their impact that deters me. I am not much for that stinging feeling and so I always feel a little uneasy delivering it.

I do consider myself competent with a flogger and truly enjoy delivering a good flogging to an eager bottom. Most of the time when I play, my partner is someone who identifies as a bottom or a "switch" (someone who can easily take on either the role of a Top or bottom). That is most of the time….

My big exception to this is a strange ritual a good friend and devilishly evil Top started many years ago. Ms P and I have been friends for many years. We first discovered each other at a local leather bar here in Dallas. She was there with her boy, a handsome man in his mid-thirties who set off my "gaydar" almost immediately. That intrigued me. Here was what appeared to be a straight woman with a gay "boy" in tow. Additionally it seemed that most of the club's other patrons regarded her and her boy as a novelty. They kept a respectful distance.

I watched here for several nights, noting the interaction between her and her boy and the elegantly formal manner of his service to her. She and her boy had all the earmarks of "old guard" leather with the exception of her gender. Finally, my curiosity got the best of me and I approached her. I think it was the fact that she smoked cigars that gave me the opportunity to break the ice.

Once I introduced myself, Ms P and I immediately struck up a lively conversation. She was clever and light hearted, yet she could turn on an aura of old guard Top that could send the bravest man away with a simple look. As our friendship grew, I came to understand her complex personality. She was a lesbian Top with a gay man as her boy. Their relationship was very deep and his service to her was both respectful and loving.

Once we got to know each other better, I had a chance to see Ms P in action at a play party. She was wicked and strong with a penchant for physical scenes. She loved flogging, and for a small woman, only 5 feet tall, she was surprisingly strong. More than once I saw her bring a bottom to his or her knees during a scene.

After a couple of years, she and I were attending an event out of town together. Having no one to play with at the event's dungeon party, we decided to trade floggings with each other.

Again, I found out just how strong she was. Also, I found she enjoyed the same style of flogging as me. I like to deliver a "thuddy" flogging, bringing as many of the floggers tails into contact with the back of my partner as possible. The effect is like being hit with a heavy bag of sand. The force of the flogger comes into contact with the full area of the back and shoulders and really packs a wallop.

I returned the favor with a similar scene with her. What was interesting aside from the nice sensations of the scene was the effect it had on the crowd in the dungeon. They knew us both as Tops and in their limited world view, Tops didn't get flogged!

Both Ms P and I were delighted to broaden the vision of that group, and later as we were chatting and decompressing from the scenes, we laughed at the strange looks people had given us.

These traded floggings eventually became a yearly event. Ms P and I would always manage to be at an event together and decide it was time for the "annual beating". Most of the time these were just good fun, and left us both with warm backs and a good endorphin rush. However, one year stands out in my memory as special.

We were at a party given by a large play group in central Texas. After I got a nice good thuddy beating from Ms P, she took off her vest and shirt and turned to offer me her back.I had recovered sufficiently from my flogging and started to warm her up a little by doing some mild whipping with a very soft and sensuous elk hide flogger I have.

I kept my strokes to the meaty parts of her back. Avoiding the lower back where blows could damage her kidneys and the center of her spine. After a few minutes of warm up, to get the blood flowing in her skin and make her ready for heavier blows she turned her head and looked me square in the eye.

"Are you sure you know how to use that thing?" she said.

That stopped me in mid swing and I waited a moment to process what she had said. In that few seconds of silence I heard at least one sharp intake of breath from an onlooker and then realized that Ms P was trying to egg me on.

"Well I guess I had better get in some practice." I said as I put my full weight into the next blow.

The noise of the elk hide against her skin made a loud whack. I watched her back contract from the force of the blow and he shake off the sensation.

"Well that's better," she said with a slight grimace, "but you kinda hit like a girl."

At that remark, I knew what she wanted, and I tossed my elk hide flogger aside and pulled out my heaviest bull hide one. This one was special and had been made for me by one of the countries legendary whip makers.

"Well, "I replied. "better turn your head back around Missy, because I am ready to get started for real."

I heard her laugh as she turned toward the St. Andrew's Cross and grabbed the beams.

My next blows were measured but strong, working first one shoulder and then the other. I kept my rhythm steady to let her process the sensation and anticipate the next blow. This steady pounding continued for a few minutes until her back was bright red.

I approached her and ran my fingernails down the skin of her back lightly, knowing it would send a wave of pain through her body. She groaned and then turned again to meet my gaze.

"Well that was a little better, but I still have to wonder what you are holding back for?"

She was taunting me again and by now the people watching us were muttering. The scene of two Tops playing was unusual enough, but they were not used to seeing someone who was being flogged be sassy and defiant with the person doing the flogging. I guess they were going to have their leather-world view broadened a bit.

I started in on her back again. Measuring my blows, but working from the side so as much of the flogger as possible would impact her shoulders and back at the same time. These strikes were much more powerful and began leaving distinct marks where the tails of the whip landed.

She was writhing and almost dancing under the sensations. I had guessed she really needed this catharsis. Only a year or so before her boy had passed away from complications of HIV/AIDS, and though she had grieved, sometimes just having a physical release is what you need.

This whole time she had been wearing high heeled boots. And she almost seemed to be dancing under the blows of my whip. I paused for a moment and she did something that I couldn't ignore. She wiggled her ass at me, and though we had not negotiated anything regarding her buttocks, I couldn't resist the target.

I took a good swing landing the full force of the heavy bull hide on her right cheek.

"Yeow!" She wailed.

"Yeow is not a safe word," I admonished her and delivered a matching blow to the other cheek.

"We didn't negotiate a spanking!" She yelped, as she continued to wiggle her ass.

"Funny, I thought you sticking your butt out was negotiation enough."

With that I gave her a fast series of lashes to each cheek, ending with a blow from the side that caught both of them in one swat.

She held on to the cross and almost climbed up off the floor. It was so absolutely slapstick that I burst out laughing. When she finally climbed down, I figured she had enough and she turned and fell into my arms. We hugged for a few minutes and then I sat her down on the floor with me.

We were both covered in sweat and giggling like children. The scene was one of the best I have ever had, and though it was not erotic, it was playful and filled with childlike energy.

The next week she showed me pictures of her butt and back. It was bruised black and blue with a slight tint of yellow and green. I told her it was in honor of Gay Pride that I turned her backside into a rainbow.

In Conclusion

I like to tell stories. I think our stories are vital to who we are as kinky people. In tribal societies their stories are the way they pass history on to future generations. We in the Leather/fetish/BDSM community, the community I call kinky, are a tribe. We have our own rituals, our own sacred spaces and our own history. Though we are all part of other sexual groups, gay, straight, lesbian, bisexual, transgendered and part of many other groups social, political, religious and secular, we are part of the same tribe.

Our collective memory lives in stories of our experiences and those of our friends. As we tell those stories, it is not hard to imagine us gathered around a campfire instead of a table in a café. Sharing these stories continues the creation of our mythology, and that is vital to our existence. Myths are not fictional stories; they are tales that contain an underlying truth. The actual people and events may be exaggerated or romanticized, but the key points of the stories impart wisdom. It is that wisdom that sustains us and enriches our community.

I sincerely hope that my contribution through these stories can in some way add to our common mythology. Though I have consciously changed the names and places involved, I have left the truth unvarnished. All these scenes were real and the people in them all contribute to that wisdom. For their parts of these stories I will always be grateful.

As to the title, *Playing with Pain*, it reflects the seed of truth in all my experiences. Pain can be a beginning or an end in itself. It can be a simple diversion, or a doorway to a spiritual experience. Pain can be part of a scene, or part of a ritual that transcends the conventional BDSM play and becomes something much more. Pain in all its many forms can be an awakening to a greater reality.

To those who say, "I'm not into pain", I ask the question, "How can you know pleasure?"

Hardy Haberman

A BDSM Glossary

When I first began writing this book, I assumed it would be of interest to people already familiar with the BDSM scene. I must remind myself that some people who read this might not have any knowledge or even exposure to the BDSM scene and might need a few definitions to help decipher the text. I have previously printed a similar glossary in my book, *More Family Jewels, Further Explorations in Male Genitorture. (2007, Nazca Plains Publishing)*

In the kinky world, we use a lot of jargon that could be easily misinterpreted by those unfamiliar with our language. So in the interest of better communication and to avoid any confusion here are a few terms I use in the book.

BDSM – an acronym most often representing Bondage, Discipline (BD) and Sadomasochism (SM). Some people also include Dominance and Submission (DS) giving the middle two letters different meaning. When I use it I am always referring to consensual activity between adults. These terms and or their derivatives will appear often as a short hand to avoid the inevitable tongue twisting that comes from spelling them out fully.

GLBT – (Not a sandwich!) Another acronym standing for Gay Lesbian Bisexual Transgender. Again it avoids overly verbose sentences.

The Scene – I use this term to speak of the BDSM community. It also includes pretty much all kinky activities included in the leather/fetish area.

Lifestyle – I loathe this word and will use it only in quotations. It refers to the BDSM scene as well, but I personally do not consider what I do a lifestyle, it is my life. Lifestyle, to me is indicative of a trendy passing fad kind of interest, and my kink is not a passing fad.

Kink – A term referring to sexual activity that is outside the most ordinary and unadventurous kind. It can also refer to almost all activities in the BDSM scene.

Kinky – adjective referring to the activities described above and the texture of my pubic hair.

Vanilla – referring to a person who is not part of the BDSM or kink community. I understand it also can be a flavor of ice cream.

Leather – sometimes referring to a fetish for leather garments and accessories, also referring to BDSM activities in general.

Leatherman – a male member of the Leather or BDSM Community. The term comes from the gay community but is now used to refer to any male identified individual in the scene. It has no role connotation of dominance or submission. Traditionally, a Leatherman wears leather: chaps, vests, boots, harnesses, etc. These are all symbols as well as fetish clothing that can immediately indicate his preferences. The image of the Leatherman has been iconized by artists such as Tom of Finland.

Top – The dominant participant in an SM activity. Most often used by gay men to indicate who is in control of the scene or who is in the dominant role in a sexual coupling. In text this term is usually capitalized to indicate the dominant role.

bottom – Referring to the passive or submissive role in an SM scene. A person can "bottom" in a scene without being submissive. Bottoming is an activity that would include receiving the effects of an activity such as flogging or spanking. In text this term is usually not capitalized to indicate the submissive role.

Dom or Domme – The masculine and feminine terms used for a person in a dominant role in a DS scene. (Both are pronounced "dahm", Domme is a French derivative and the "me" ending is silent. This is a pet peeve for me since many people pronounce the feminine word as "dah-mey". Sacré bleu!)

Sub or subbie – referring to the person playing a submissive role in a DS scene. The diminutive "subbie" is used often by Dommes in reference to their partners as a term of endearment.

Play – the activities that take place during a BDSM session. Flogging, spanking, bondage, etc. Originally these were referred to as "work" by early gay Leathermen but the term has fallen out of favor.

Player – any participant in the BDSM/Leather/Fetish activities. People involved in a scene are referred to as players.

Scene Name – for kinky people who are in the closet or feel they must remain anonymous many use assumed names in the community. This is a source of both endless amusement and endless confusion. What started as simple nom de plumes has become a morass of odd names and titles. Though I personally have never used a scene name, I respect people who do, and try to call them whatever they want in public.

Daddy – not referring to my father. This is a title used by some leathermen and even women as not only their honorific but a role they play in either their relationship or in the community. Many people play "Daddy/boy" scenes. These have nothing to do with child abuse; they are roles taken on by the partners and are far too involved to go into here. There are also some who play Daddy/girl or Mommy/girl or boy.

Master – You will see this honorific thrown around a lot in the BDSM community. It is a title used for a person who has a "slave". I prefer to reserve that title for the slave to use for his or her Master. That said, there are people who are known as "Master (insert name here)" in the community and it serves as their scene name. A few people are commonly called Master by the community and this usually denotes their standing as a respected member of the community. Again, it's all very complex and could be the subject of another book by itself.

slave – a person who voluntarily takes on the role of someone "owned" by another. Many times slaves and Masters have contracts that spell out their obligations and property rights specifically, other times it is a casual relationship. The Master/slave community has grown recently and is already the subject of several good books on the subject.

Dungeon – (also referred to as a playspace) a space designed for BDSM activities. This can be a room in an individual's house that is reserved for play, or a large space open to members of a club or the public at large. Public dungeons are not really "public". In almost all cases for legal reasons, they are open to members only or guests of members. Whenever I speak of public play, I am referring to play in this kind of space. Anyone entering a dungeon knows that will be seeing BDSM activities. A dungeon is a consensual space.

Safe, sane and consensual – a motto first used to describe what members of the BDSM community do in private. It has become a guideline for BDSM play that helps protect everyone involved. As with almost every aspect of BDSM, the terms are somewhat subjective. Here is my take on them:

> *Safe* - an activity that does not present a risk to the health of the players.
> *Sane* - all activities that are undertaken in a reasonably sane state of mind.
> *Consensual* - all activities involve the full informed consent of everyone involved.
> (This is why a Dungeon is a consensual space, even though I may refer to it as a public playspace.)

This is not intended to be a definitive glossary of terms but it should be sufficient to give someone who is not familiar with our activities a basic understanding of the terminology. Also, this is the way I use these terms. Others may differ on their definitions, but that is a whole different discussion.

If all this is a bit too much for you, put the book down for a while and then pick it up once you recover. For many people the first time they are exposed to the BDSM/Leather/fetish world they are overwhelmed. It's understandable. BDSM challenges the whole paradigm of modern life. It looks at the world and relationships in a vastly different and frank way and that can be unsettling. The good news is it can also be one of the most freeing experiences you can ever have.

About the Author

Since the mid-70's Hardy has been an active in the leather community and a member of many BDSM/Fetish organizations including Dallas Motorcycle Club, Leather Rose Society, NLA-Dallas, Discipline Corps and a founding member of Inquisition-Dallas. Considering himself a "Pain Technologist" he specializes in CBT and has an unusual fondness for clips clamps and clothespins, as well as more esoteric SM play.

Professionally he is a filmmaker. His documentary on the leather lifestyle "LEATHER" has won numerous awards and appeared in festivals around the world, and his latest film, "Out of the Darkness, The Reality of SM" is currently being used by health care professionals around the world. His non-leather projects include the documentary "The Big Fair" a look inside the State Fair of Texas, which is soon to be distributed.

Outside his filmmaking, he is a gay political activist, author & speaker on aspects of the SM/Leather scene. His first book "The Family Jewels, A guide to male genital play and torment" is available at bookstores everywhere.

He was awarded NLAI's *Man of the Year* award in 1999 and in 2007 he was honored with a *Lifetime Achievement Award* from the National

Leather Association International. Since April, 1995, he and his boy Patrick have been living together in Dallas with their Feline Mistresses, Elvira and Samantha and newcomer Jack-The-Cat.

Hardy Haberman is also the Author of:

The Family Jewels: A Guide to Male Genital Play and Torment.
(2001, Greenery Press)

More Family Jewels, Further Explorations in Male Genitorture.
(2007, Nazca Plains Publishing)

www.ingramcontent.com/pod-product-compliance
Lightning Source LLC
Chambersburg PA
CBHW052217270326
41931CB00011B/2387